Where God Leads,

I Will Follow

Devotional Journal

BARBOUR
PUBLISHING

"For I know the plans I have for you," declares the LORD, "plans to prosper you and not to harm you, plans to give you hope and a future."

JEREMIAH 29:11

Introduction

What does it mean to follow Jesus? The cost is steep, but the reward is staggering. The journey is fraught with mountaintops and valleys, but Jesus walks alongside us. When we're too weary to stumble forward, He strengthens us. Jesus said, "Whoever wants to be my disciple must deny themselves and take up their cross and follow me. For whoever wants to save their life will lose it, but whoever loses their life for me will find it. What good will it be for someone to gain the whole world, yet forfeit their soul? . . . For the Son of Man is going to come in his Father's glory" (Matthew 16:24–27).

May these ninety devotionals inspire you to lose yourself and gain the richness of Christ. He offers life, rest, and victory to those who are willing to follow Him. Run after Jesus. He's waiting for you.

Count the Cost

*I consider that our present sufferings are not worth
comparing with the glory that will be revealed in us.*

Romans 8:18

M ake sure you know what you're getting into." Any time we make a decision
that could greatly alter the course of our lives someone is bound to offer this
advice. Jesus also cautioned the crowds trailing Him not to take up His cause lightly.

In Luke 14 Jesus tells of a builder who wisely estimates the cost of the tower
he wants to construct to determine whether he can afford to complete it. Jesus
warns that laying the foundation without adequate funds will lead to ridicule
when the builder is unable to finish.

As disciples of Christ we aren't promised trouble-free or even comfortable lives,
but He does offer something more satisfying. Jesus asked that we surrender our
will in exchange for His peace. But His peace isn't like the counterfeit confidence
we manufacture. His peace radiates into our souls like warm sunshine regardless of
the storms howling around us. And with His peace He offers more than the whole
world, He holds out eternity.

The apostle Paul had done his due diligence. He said, "For to me, to live is
Christ and to die is gain" (Philippians 1:21). He knew that in life he could further
expand God's kingdom, but in death he would gain heaven and forever be with his
Lord. He didn't allow the temporary pleasures of this fleeting life to render him
spiritually nearsighted.

Giving it all up to follow Jesus might seem like a foolishly high price to pay in the
world's eyes, because the world serves the gods of wealth, power, and ego. But Paul
knew that "God was pleased through the foolishness of what was preached to save
those who believe" (1 Corinthians 1:21). Choosing to be a servant in the Master's
castle rather than building our own empires will always seem foolish to the world.

Have you counted the cost? Are you willing to stick with Jesus no matter the
price? Consider wisely. Your eternity hangs in the balance.

Pass the Salt

"It is an everlasting covenant of salt before the
Lord for both you and your offspring."
Numbers 18:19

"Hmm. Needs a tad more salt." Nobody likes bland food. We sprinkle—or dump—salt on just about everything because it tastes better after it has been seasoned. Salt can mingle with the flavors of other foods and enrich their savory appeal because it retains its original form even when combined with other substances. When you dash a little salt into your soup, it's still salt!

In ancient times salt was valued for more than just its flavor-enhancing properties. Without refrigerators, salt was an important preservative necessary to keep food from spoiling. Salt was such a hot commodity that it was used as currency. Roman soldiers were often paid in salt; this practice led to our word *salary*.

Because of its unique attributes God required the Old Testament Israelites to salt their sacrifices. His covenants were sealed with salt. "Season all your grain offerings with salt. Do not leave the salt of the covenant of your God out of your grain offerings; add salt to all your offerings" (Leviticus 2:13). Salt's unchanging, purifying nature symbolizes the eternal, abiding quality of God's covenant with the Israelites and reflects His own steadfast character and faithfulness.

Sin offerings were given to atone for wrongdoing. "Offer a male goat without defect for a sin offering. . . . Sprinkle salt on them and sacrifice them as a burnt offering to the Lord" (Ezekiel 43:22, 24). But Jesus became the final sin offering by dying on the cross. "For he bore the sin of many, and made intercession for the transgressors" (Isaiah 53:12).

And in light of this covenant Jesus encouraged the New Testament believers, "You are the salt of the earth" (Matthew 5:13). His final sacrifice is salted with the everlasting hope and promise of the Gospel message that we, His followers, spread to the world. As salt we must remain uninfluenced by the world and fulfill our task to preserve and purify humankind by showing them the way to Jesus' saving grace.

Those Kooky Prophets

The LORD sent prophets to the people to bring them back to him.

2 CHRONICLES 24:19

Nothing churns up the rumor mill like your average Joe doing something bizarre. The whole neighborhood turns out to speculate on his sanity and whisper, "What on earth is he thinking?" And let's admit it; God's Old Testament prophets definitely weren't afraid to walk on the weird side and really give the people something fantastic to gossip about.

The prophets were so dedicated to getting God's message out that they were willing to do just about anything to bring people back to obedience to God—and they did some straight up strange stuff. We'd probably draw the line at walking around naked and barefoot for three years, or lying on one side for 390 days (that's over a year, people!), marrying a prostitute, or how about shaving our heads or eating wild honey (okay, not so bad) and locusts (umm, could we get fries with that instead?).

God had a stubborn and rebellious nation on His hands, and He needed to make a statement they wouldn't forget. But it took some pretty crazy stuff to get their attention. God wants everyone to hear His Word. The apostle Peter said that "the Lord is not slow in keeping his promise. . . . Instead he is patient with you, not wanting anyone to perish, but everyone to come to repentance" (2 Peter 3:9).

Today God is still dealing with His stubborn, rebellious children. But how willing are we, Christ's followers, to stand out so others can see God's love? Are we more concerned with our reputations than we are with saving their souls? Now God probably isn't going to ask us to walk around without clothes (whew!), but He does ask us to live out His love in front of our neighbors, coworkers, friends, and family. Take a chance today and don't "conform to the pattern of this world, but be transformed by the renewing of your mind" (Romans 12:2).

On the Run

Where can I go from your Spirit? Where can I flee from your presence?
PSALM 139:7

There she goes again. Toddlers all seem to go through a stage of fleeing from correction. They're happily pulling everything from Mom's purse or playing in her makeup—until she catches them. Once they realize their mistake, their first inclination is to grab the goods and run. Their escape efforts are futile. Mom is bigger and faster. She will catch them eventually.

It's equally ridiculous when we try to escape God. Whether we've done something we know He doesn't condone or we're rebelling against His plan for us, there's nowhere He can't find us.

We could save ourselves a lot of pain and heartache if we'd run back to God instead of away from Him when we mess up. The prodigal son in Luke 15 had wasted all of his money, and he became so hungry he was ready to eat pig slop before he came to his senses.

Maybe we fear that God is waiting to punish us if we crawl back to Him. But like the father of that wayward, stubborn son, God is eagerly watching for our return so He can celebrate our homecoming. "While he was still a long way off, his father saw him and was filled with compassion for him; he ran to his son, threw his arms around him and kissed him" (Luke 15:20). That definitely doesn't sound like an angry parent.

This boy had taken his inheritance prematurely and squandered it, but when he realized how wrong he'd been he swallowed his pride and hightailed it home. But his father wasn't waiting to gloat over his foolishness; instead he *ran* to his son and threw a huge party to celebrate his repentance. " 'For this son of mine was dead and is alive again; he was lost and is found' " (Luke 15:24).

Have you been on the run, afraid to face God in the aftermath of your failures? Set your GPS toward home. Your heavenly Father is waiting to gather you in His arms.

Unfinished

"This third I will put into the fire; I will refine them like silver and test them like gold. They will call on my name and I will answer them."

ZECHARIAH 13:9

❦

"Diamonds are a girl's best friend." We're all familiar with this popular adage. Women have always been attracted to the sparkling beauty of precious stones. But these gems are more than just pretty baubles. Formed a hundred miles below the earth's surface, diamonds require intense heat and crushing pressure to grow.

Diamonds also have some unique attributes. Their rigorous creation transforms them into the hardest known natural material on earth. As such, diamonds can survive in extreme surroundings that would destroy other materials. They can withstand severe physical, chemical, and even radioactive forces. Pure diamond is also the most transparent material known. It reflects light from the ultraviolet, visible, and infrared spectrums.

But diamonds don't come out of the earth looking like the polished, cut stones we find in our jewelry. A diamond in the rough can look like a small, ordinary stone. Most people would probably overlook it completely, not recognizing its potential value.

Sometimes we wonder why God seems to be trying us, allowing us to struggle. But just as diamonds must endure extreme conditions while growing into durable, glittering gems, God is working to transform us. He's purifying our hearts so we can reflect Christ. "And the God of all grace, who called you to his eternal glory in Christ, after you have suffered a little while, will himself restore you and make you strong, firm and steadfast" (1 Peter 5:10).

We may not always understand why things happen, but when we are walking in God's will we can trust Him to use us for His purposes. His goodwill toward us isn't clouded by selfish motives. "And we know that in all things God works for the good of those who love him, who have been called according to his purpose" (Romans 8:28).

God isn't finished with you yet. Endure His polishing with the hope of obtaining eternal beauty.

Beware the Yeast

"Every grain offering you bring to the LORD must be made without yeast, for you are not to burn any yeast or honey in a food offering presented to the LORD."
LEVITICUS 2:11

Few things arouse our taste buds and get our salivary glands gushing like the yeasty smell of baking bread. Bakers know the secret to their airy pastries is yeast. Yeast is a fungus that multiplies rapidly when it consumes sugar and then emits carbon dioxide, which fluffs the bread. A tiny amount, about a quarter ounce, can raise a whole loaf of bread.

So why was God opposed to the presence of this mini miracle-maker in His sacrifices? God has nothing against yeast; He used it to represent sin. Just as a little of this microorganism will alter a whole lump of dough, seemingly small and inconsequential sins can have devastating effects on our lives. The unleavened bread also pointed toward the sinless life of Christ, who said, "I am the bread of life" (John 6:35).

Jesus warned His disciples that others would try to lead them astray with flawed teaching. " 'Be on your guard against the yeast of the Pharisees' " (Matthew 16:6). Just as Satan orchestrated the downfall of the entire human race with a few carefully placed deceptions, one wrong person can infect many. The apostle Paul cautioned, "A little yeast works through the whole batch of dough" (Galatians 5:9).

Once we're aware of the insidious nature of sin, we have to actively weed it from our thoughts and actions. Paul advised that we "test everything that is said. Hold on to what is good" (1 Thessalonians 5:21 NLT). We can't take everything we hear at face value. We must search the scriptures regularly so we can discern truth from Satan's lies.

Sometimes we convince ourselves that small indiscretions or little white lies don't matter. But Jesus called us to a better life. Any and all sin will corrode our integrity and blind us to what's right. Are any "small" and "harmless" sins flourishing in your life?

Treasure Seeker

Why spend money on what is not bread,
and your labor on what does not satisfy?
Isaiah 55:2

A glowing tree. The promise of good things held within shiny, ribbon-enwrapped packages. Tables overflowing with iced cookies and cakes. Children spend 364 days each year anticipating Christmas Day with innocent wonder. Their excitement is infectious, spreading joy throughout their families.

How would it affect the kingdom of God if we looked to heaven with the same insatiable delight? Jesus said, "The kingdom of heaven is like treasure hidden in a field. When a man found it, he hid it again, and then in his joy went and sold all he had and bought that field" (Matthew 13:44). When living *forever* with Jesus is our reward, our joyful expectation of this gift should propel us to sell out for Him.

Follow the apostle Paul's lead and catch the thrill of heaven: "Whatever were gains to me I now consider loss for the sake of Christ. . . . I want to know Christ—yes, to know the power of his resurrection. . . . Forgetting what is behind and straining toward what is ahead, I press on toward the goal to win the prize for which God has called me heavenward in Christ Jesus" (Philippians 3:7, 10, 13–14). Our enthusiasm for Christ will overwhelm our desire for temporary comfort and pleasure when our focus is fixed on our glorious future.

Jesus taught that we should store our treasures in heaven rather than on earth where they can easily be destroyed or stolen. Our obedience to God and the kingdom work we complete on earth will give us great things to look forward to in heaven. Jesus knew that "where your treasure is, there your heart will be also" (Matthew 6:21). And He wants our undivided devotion.

Eternal life with God is a gem of incalculable value. We can fritter away our time, effort, and money on ephemeral things, but as MasterCard would say, a new sweater—$40.00; a spa day—$300.00; eternity with God—priceless.

Where is your treasure?

Satisfied

*As the deer pants for streams of water, so my soul pants for you,
my God. My soul thirsts for God, for the living God.*
PSALM 42:1–2

She hurried toward the town well in the heat of the noon sun. She darted a glance over her shoulder and sighed. *Good, I can draw my water in peace.* Her guilt weighed as heavily on her shoulders as the water jar she carried. She'd been through numerous husbands, but it never worked out. She'd finally abandoned married life and decided to try a live-in boyfriend. After all, why should this relationship be any different? Something was always missing.

As she neared the well, she saw a man sitting beside it. She hesitated. He was a Jew. He would never suffer the presence of a woman like her, let alone a *Samaritan* woman. But she was thirsty. And she'd waited for the other women to finish so she wouldn't have to endure their whispered slurs.

She hurried forward, but her mouth dropped open when He asked her for a drink. "You are a Jew and I am a Samaritan woman. How can you ask me for a drink?" she whispered.

The man's eyes met hers, and His piercing gaze seemed to search her secrets. "If you knew the gift of God and who it is that asks you for a drink, you would have asked him and he would have given you living water," Jesus told her. "Everyone who drinks this water will be thirsty again, but whoever drinks the water I give them will never thirst. Indeed, the water I give them will become in them a spring of water welling up to eternal life" (John 4:10, 13–14).

Are you dying of thirst? Searching for more? Just as the deer depend on cool streams for life, our eternal lives depend on the living waters of Jesus. He sees us try over and over to satisfy our cravings with empty pleasure. And He offers to fulfill our deepest need—a new life in Christ. He satisfies our thirst.

The Coal Yard

If your enemy is hungry, give him food to eat; if he is thirsty, give him water to drink. In doing this, you will heap burning coals on his head, and the LORD will reward you.

PROVERBS 25:21–22

There's an old story about a boy named Joe Benton.[1] He and his friends were planning to sail their new boat in the creek on a sunny Saturday. But when they arrived at the water, they found the boat ruined.

Joe knew that nasty Fritz Brown was the culprit, and he plotted his revenge. He set up a trip string along the path and sat down to wait. But before Fritz came, Joe's cousin Herbert strolled down the path. He saw Joe's setup and asked what he was doing. With a knowing smile Herbert offered Joe a better payback. "How would you like to put a few coals of fire on his head?"

Ecstatic, Joe wanted to know exactly how to execute this plan. But Herbert merely quoted Proverbs 25:21–22. Joe was crestfallen when he realized that he'd have to be nice to the one who'd destroyed his boat. Herbert hinted that Fritz didn't have the money to buy books while Joe had a large library.

The next time Joe saw Fritz he decided to give those hot coals a try and offered to loan Fritz his new book. In the end Joe discovered how effective his kindness could be—he gained a new friend who also repaired his boat.

"And Joe found out afterwards that the more he used of this curious kind of coal, the larger supply he had on hand—kind thoughts, kind words, and kind actions. 'I declare, Cousin Herbert,' said he, with a strange twinkle in his eye, 'I think I shall have to set up a coal yard.'"

Do you reserve your kindness for only your friends? Imagine the shocked reaction you'd get for complimenting someone who has just insulted you. Get to it! Heap on those coals.

---

1. Society of Friends. New York Yearly Meeting. Central Tract Committee, "Joe Benton's Coal Yard" (1878).

Vanity Fair

I considered all that my hands had done and the toil I had expended in doing it, and behold, all was vanity. . .there was nothing to be gained under the sun.

<small>ECCLESIASTES 2:11 ESV</small>

John Bunyan's Christian, of *The Pilgrim's Progress*, reached the city of Vanity on his journey toward the Celestial City. The town held a year-round market called Vanity Fair. "At this fair are all such merchandise sold as houses, lands, trades. . .titles, countries, kingdoms, lusts, pleasures; and delights of all sorts, such as harlots, wives, husbands, children, masters, servants, lives, blood, bodies, souls, silver, gold, precious stones, and what not."

Christian and his friend Faithful unwittingly entered a community interested only in self-gratification, commerce, and affluence. Any desire could be bought and sold at the fair. When asked what they would purchase, the friends said that they were only interested in truth. The townspeople ridiculed them as lunatics and threw them in jail for disrupting the fair.

Our modern culture bears a striking resemblance to Vanity Fair. With the ease of internet shopping and the torrent of advertisements spewed from our TVs, the world peddles every pleasure imaginable. Don't like your looks? Try this miracle makeup. Want a new boyfriend? We'll pair you up online with sophisticated matching software. If you desire it, you can purchase it.

But the one thing the Vanity Fair didn't deal in was truth. They found the idea so disruptive to their lifestyle that they imprisoned Christian just for seeking it. Jesus knew that His disciples also would not be accepted. Before His crucifixion He prayed, "They do not belong to this world any more than I do. . . . Teach them your word, which is truth" (John 17:16–17 NLT).

Are you seeking truth or vanity? As followers of Jesus we are to "make no provision for the flesh, to gratify its desires" (Romans 13:14 ESV). If you've been beguiled by the merchandise of Vanity Fair, echo this prayer today: "Turn my eyes from worthless things, and give me life through your word" (Psalm 119:37 NLT).

Weigh Your Emotions

Those who trust in themselves are fools,
but those who walk in wisdom are kept safe.
PROVERBS 28:26

Emotion is a formidable force, and excellent storytelling evokes it from the audience. The characters' passions compel us—triumph, tragedy, outrage, love, betrayal.

But like any power, emotion should be treated with caution. Our emotions don't always tell the truth—they can be quite deceptive. In *The Lord of the Rings* trilogy, a dangerous ring of power has been found. It bears the ominous inscription "One ring to rule them all. One ring to find them. One ring to bring them all and in the darkness bind them." This ring twists desires—it manipulates, it seduces with power. Those who succumb to its temptation are overshadowed by jealousy, rage, and control.

The wizard Gandalf recoils when Frodo the hobbit demands that he take the ring. "Don't tempt me. . . . I would use this ring from a desire to do good. But through me it would wield a power too great and terrible to imagine." At times our emotions can convince us that evil is good. The world shouts, "If it feels good, do it!" But just as the ring warped their good intentions, our hearts can manipulate us with self-fulfilling feelings. God warns us to beware: "The heart is deceitful above all things and beyond cure" (Jeremiah 17:9).

So how do we protect ourselves from emotional manipulation? Thankfully God has sent us some help. "The person with the Spirit makes judgments about all things, but such a person is not subject to merely human judgments. . . .We have the mind of Christ" (1 Corinthians 2:15–16). We can't be fooled into finding our moral compass within ourselves because our nature is sinful. We are to think like Christ, and He has given us the Bible and the Holy Spirit to guide our decisions.

Have you ever been carried away by your emotions? Knowing how someone thinks requires a deep understanding of that person's character, priorities, and goals. Do you know Jesus well enough to think like Him?

Be Still

"The Lord will fight for you; you need only to be still."
EXODUS 14:14

———————

F ailure to trust—we've all stumbled over it at one time or another. It's tempting to judge the Old Testament Israelites harshly for their fickle habits, but unfortunately we mirror their faithless ways more than we care to admit. God literally plagued the Egyptian people until they cast the Israelites out of their land and gladly handed over their wealth just to see the dust from the Israeli caravan fading in the distance. Now that's wearing out your welcome! But still Israel doubted Him.

If we're honest, we're just like God's ragtag bunch of forgetful two-timers. We read about His past wonders and we experience His transforming power and blessing on our lives, but when we see trouble on the horizon, we quake with fear and complain.

Trapped against the sea and the mountains, the Israelites were terrified when the Egyptian army pursued them: "Was it because there were no graves in Egypt that you brought us to the desert to die?" they accused Moses. "It would have been better for us to serve the Egyptians than to die in the desert!" (Exodus 14:11–12). God was delivering them from generations of bondage, and yet at the first sign of trouble they abandoned their faith and screamed to be taken back into slavery. But Moses said, "Do not be afraid. Stand firm and you will see the deliverance the Lord will bring you today.... The Lord will fight for you; you need only to be still" (Exodus 14:13–14).

The Israelites were trapped—or so they thought. But no situation in our lives is hopeless for our God who can deliver us in unexpected ways. Most likely none of their battle strategies included dividing the waters of the Red Sea and strolling through like nobody's business. When life throws you a startling curve, or even when you see a crisis approaching, don't despair. Trust God. Be still. Because His "power is made perfect in weakness" (2 Corinthians 12:9).

Mistaken Identity

He will delight in obeying the LORD. He will not judge by
appearance nor make a decision based on hearsay.

ISAIAH 11:3 NLT

"How despicably I have acted...I, who have prided myself on my discernment! On the very beginning of our acquaintance, I have courted prepossession and ignorance, and driven reason away." Miss Elizabeth Bennet from Jane Austen's *Pride and Prejudice* has just realized the degree to which she has misjudged Mr. Darcy, and her humiliation is complete.

We've all been there. We meet someone and instantly dislike him or her for some trivial reason—an insult, real or imagined, or the person's clothes, language, or tattoos. We make snap judgments about the person's character and congratulate ourselves on our discernment.

Jesus warns us repeatedly against judging others, and prejudice is one of its worst forms—we base our opinion on preconceived ideas formed before we know the first real fact about someone. " 'Do not judge, or you too will be judged. For in the same way you judge others, you will be judged, and with the measure you use, it will be measured to you' " (Matthew 7:1–2).

Prejudice creates unnecessary divisions among God's children. Our heavenly Father created each and every one of us, and parents don't tolerate unfounded hatred of their children. " 'Truly I understand that God shows no partiality, but in every nation anyone who fears him and does what is right is acceptable to him' " (Acts 10:34–35 ESV).

It's impossible to introduce others to Jesus when we're carrying around bigotry and judgment. It's our responsibility to share the Gospel message with our family, our friends and neighbors, the grocery store clerk, the homeless guy on the corner—to be Jesus to the world. And prejudice wasn't part of Jesus' message: "God did not send his Son into the world to condemn the world, but to save the world through him" (John 3:17).

Don't allow any barriers to hinder you from showing the love of Christ!

Adopted

The Spirit himself testifies with our spirit that we are God's children.
Now if we are children, then we are heirs.

ROMANS 8:16–17

M any childless couples long to adopt. Through this legal process they gain a son or daughter to love, teach, and share in their lives. But in the first-century Roman culture, the adoption process also had redemptive qualities. If a wealthy Roman citizen wanted an heir, he would adopt a young boy, often a slave, as his son.

Slaves were considered inferior and had very few rights. They were likely destined for a life of forced labor and abuse. Even slaves who attained an elevated status were still controlled by the needs of their masters.

Once he entered his new family, a child lost all ties to his old family and became a legitimate son of his new father. Any debts of the adoptee were cancelled, and he literally began a new life as his father's heir. A father could choose to disinherit his natural son, but he could never disown his adopted son. Adoptees were assured of receiving their inheritance.

As children of God our debts have been erased. We are forgiven and are no longer bound as slaves to sin! We can celebrate our certain future of eternal life in heaven with our Father. It is now our privilege and responsibility as an adopted child of God to be led by the Spirit. "God sent his Son, born of a woman, born under the law, to redeem those under the law, that we might receive adoption to sonship. Because you are his sons, God sent the Spirit of his Son into our hearts, the Spirit who calls out, '*Abba*, Father' " (Galatians 4:4–6).

In a beautiful display of His love and mercy God sacrificed His beloved Son to make our redemption possible. The apostle Paul confirms that as adoptees we too are "God's chosen ones, holy and beloved" (Colossians 3:12 ESV).

God has replaced our slavery with sonship. Consider for a moment that you are a beloved child of God.

Press On

*I don't mean to say that I have already achieved these things or
that I have already reached perfection. But I press on to possess
that perfection for which Christ Jesus first possessed me.*
PHILIPPIANS 3:12 NLT

How do we follow Jesus? When He called the twelve disciples, Jesus didn't ask for a shallow investment or a halfhearted commitment. He asked them to leave *everything* behind and follow Him. What phenomenon caused full-grown men to walk away from life as they knew it? What promise did they hear in His voice that convinced them they needed to know more?

Our goal, like His first disciples, should be to know Christ more. He walked the earth and provided us with the perfect example of how to treat one another. He showed us exactly the kind of influence we should be on the world around us. We need look no further than our Savior to find the perfect role model.

Jesus' message was stunning in its novelty. Popular wisdom was overturned, and a new standard was laid: Love the ones who hate you. Don't judge, instead forgive. Don't treat people as they treat you, but as you want to be treated. Die to yourself to obtain new life. Become the least and you will be the greatest. Serve to find freedom. Lose everything in order to gain it all in His kingdom.

The keys to success in God's kingdom are at odds with our experience in this fallen world. But Christ promises to remake us: "Therefore, if anyone is in Christ, the new creation has come: The old has gone, the new is here!" (2 Corinthians 5:17). We are works in progress. If we allow God to mold us, we can live new lives. We don't have to remain mired in old habits and sins.

The twelve followed Christ because He offers something bigger than money, power, or status. He gives wholeness, love, mercy, forgiveness, and life. God reforms us into His image so that Jesus can continue to walk the earth through us.

Spirit-Ripened Fruit

The fruit of the Spirit is love, joy, peace, patience, kindness,
generosity, faithfulness, gentleness, and self-control.
GALATIANS 5:22–23 NRSV

Not again. Her son's Sunday school teacher honed in on her after church. She could tell by the firm set of her jaw that James was in trouble—again. At home the exasperated mother asked her son why he was misbehaving. He ducked his head, and his thin shoulders twitched up and then down. "I try and try and try and try." He sighed heavily and threw up his hands. "I'm just not good."

Trying to be good on our own power is an exercise in frustration. The list of love, joy, peace, patience, kindness, goodness, faithfulness, gentleness, and self-control seems to mock our efforts. But Jesus warned us that we would never change our habits without Him. " 'No branch can bear fruit by itself; it must remain in the vine. Neither can you bear fruit unless you remain in me. I am the vine; you are the branches. If you remain in me and I in you, you will bear much fruit; apart from me you can do nothing' " (John 15:4–5).

We simply can't be good by ourselves. We can't attain these attributes on our own steam; they're the work of the Holy Spirit in us. What a relief that God doesn't expect us to repeatedly try and fail at work that isn't ours to do. Instead our heavenly Father asks only that we rely on the Holy Spirit to lead us. "So I say, walk by the Spirit, and you will not gratify the desires of the flesh" (Galatians 5:16).

But walking in God's Spirit does require that we hear His Word and obey it, surrendering every aspect of our lives so the Spirit's work can come to fruition. "Since we are living by the Spirit, let us follow the Spirit's leading in every part of our lives" (Galatians 5:25 NLT). In other words, we've been saved, we should act like it!

Who's Your Boss?

Whatever you do, do it all for the glory of God.
1 CORINTHIANS 10:31

Joseph rode a roller coaster of status changes. He was living it up as the favored little sib when suddenly his life took a drastic turn for the gutter. A smidge peeved at his arrogance in claiming they would all bow before him one day, his older brothers sold him into slavery.

Wow! Talk about a fall from grace. The doted-upon boy wonder was now in chains. But Joseph rose to the highest position in his master's household because "the LORD was with Joseph so that he prospered" (Genesis 39:2). Sadly, his cushy position was short lived. Falsely accused of seducing his master's wife, Joseph was slammed into prison.

But there was simply no holding Joseph down when he refused to abandon his God even as life seemed determined to defeat him. Joseph impressed the prison warden and was soon running the place. Once again God gave him success.

Joseph eventually got out of prison by helpfully interpreting some dreams for the Pharaoh, which saved all of Egypt—and his own backstabbing brothers by default—from a seven-year famine. For this he was made Pharaoh's second-in-command.

God worked out His plan for Joseph with the perspicacity of a chess master. But Joseph could have grown sullen and angry with God for some of the circumstances that assaulted him. Instead he continued to trust God and worked hard whether he was a slave in prison or one of the highest officials in the land. Long before the apostle Paul spelled out the Christian work ethic, Joseph lived it. "Whatever you do, work at it with all your heart, as working for the Lord, not for human masters" (Colossians 3:23).

Do you ever feel that some tasks are beneath you? Do you complain about your job? Remember that God has placed you there, so work for the Lord no matter how inconsequential the task. You never know what His endgame might be.

Live Victoriously

But thanks be to God! He gives us the victory through our Lord Jesus Christ.
1 CORINTHIANS 15:57

On May 8, 1945, the United States and Europe celebrated Victory in Europe Day. Nazi Germany had finally laid down its arms. Flags waved and banners flapped in the breeze. Huge crowds gathered as everyone rejoiced and danced in the streets. Fireworks ignited the evening sky where bombs once rained down destruction. More than 13,000 British prisoners of war were brought home. After long, costly years of battle, the war in Europe had finally ended. Newspaper headlines proclaimed, IT'S ALL OVER and SURRENDER IS UNCONDITIONAL.

As believers in Jesus our war with sin and death is already won. How would our daily lives change if we could muster as much enthusiasm for this victory as the citizens of Europe at the end of World War II? When Jesus took His last breath on the cross He said, "It is finished" (John 19:30). The war ended, our eternal future was secure, and Satan's surrender was unconditional.

Sin no longer has the power to enslave us. We are liberated much like the POWs. "Through Christ Jesus the law of the Spirit who gives life has set you free from the law of sin and death" (Romans 8:2). In Him we exchange oppression, defeat, and death for freedom, victory, and life.

The old hymn "Victory in Jesus" points the way:

> *I heard an old, old story, How a Savior came from glory, How He gave His life on Calvary To save a wretch like me; I heard about His groaning, Of His precious blood's atoning, Then I repented of my sins And won the victory.*

If you haven't claimed your victory through Christ, do it today. Don't keep fighting a war that's already won. Our sinful nature has been buried with Christ. We died. And now Christ lives in us. That's worth celebrating!

Buried at Sea

Who is a God like you, who pardons sin?
MICAH 7:18

Pumbaa, the repulsively lovable warthog from *The Lion King*, offered Simba this advice: "You got to put your behind in your past." Well, ineloquent maybe, but you get the idea. Many people plod joylessly along, head down, feet dragging in exhaustion because the weight of their yesterdays is crushing them bit by bit.

If this is you, there's great news! Someone has volunteered to walk beside you and carry that heavy pack for you. His name is Jesus. He offers, "Come to me, all you who are weary and burdened, and I will give you rest. . . . For my yoke is easy and my burden is light" (Matthew 11:28, 30).

We've all done things we regret. Some of us thrash ourselves over our mistakes, and at times other people like to remind us of our screw-ups too. But our heavenly Father doesn't keep a running tally of our sins so He can throw them back in our faces. Instead He chooses to forget. " 'I am he who blots out your transgressions for my own sake, and I will not remember your sins' " (Isaiah 43:25 ESV).

You can lay your worries, regrets, and guilt at the foot of the cross. You don't have to struggle under the load anymore. It doesn't matter what you've done. There's nothing He can't forgive. "*Everyone* who believes in him receives forgiveness of sins through his name" (Acts 10:43, emphasis added). But once you drop your burden, leave it when you go. We're not very good at forgiving ourselves. And it's not God's goal to lay a guilt trip on us. "This is how we know that we belong to the truth and how we set our hearts at rest in his presence: If our hearts condemn us, we know that God is greater than our hearts, and he knows everything" (1 John 3:19–20).

If you're tired and eaten by shame, release it to the One who will bury it in "the depths of the sea" (Micah 7:19). Accept His rest.

Green with Envy

For where you have envy and selfish ambition,
there you find disorder and every evil practice.

JAMES 3:16

Two sisters were in constant competition with each other. Whatever one had, the other wanted. Each regularly calculated how much their parents gave to the other and always felt that she had been slighted. The older sister was a gifted violinist who had won many accolades for her musical talents. She had been invited to perform that evening with the local symphony orchestra.

The younger sister couldn't stand the other gaining such celebrity. From the top of the stairs she watched her sister strut out the front door in her sleek black dress and heels. Her decision made, she gritted her teeth and "tripped" on the top step, breaking her arm in the fall. The entire family spent the night in the emergency room.

William Penn said, "The jealous are troublesome to others but a torment to themselves." Envy may begin with wanting what others have, but it doesn't end there. It coils its way into our hearts until we cannot "rejoice with those who rejoice" (Romans 12:15). Instead we harbor bitter hostility toward anyone who succeeds and delight in the failure and hardship of others. And worse, we destroy ourselves in the process.

The antidote to our bitter resentment is to be filled with God's contentment. The apostle Paul taught that "true godliness with contentment is itself great wealth" (1 Timothy 6:6 NLT). If we are satisfied with God's provision for us, there's no room left for envy, and we're free to be happy when good things happen to others.

Don't be discouraged if jealousy has stirred in your heart. We aren't perfect and battle constantly with our sinful nature. But God can give you a fresh perspective if you allow His peace and contentment to flood your mind. "A heart at peace gives life to the body, but envy rots the bones" (Proverbs 14:30).

Life or decay, which will you choose?

See Them

God intended it all for good. He brought me to this position so I could save the lives of many people.

GENESIS 50:20 NLT

It's said that the opposite of love is not hate but indifference. Jesus' greatest commandment is love, but in order to love others we have to see their needs. In this world of chaotic schedules and self-gratifying lifestyles we often don't lift our heads from the grindstones of our own problems and goals long enough to look around us—to see our lonely, widowed neighbor; the confused, desperate teenager who is contemplating suicide; the struggling single mom with no family to help.

A world cries out in pain just outside our doors. Many of them have physical needs that we could meet, but more importantly they're suffering without the hope of God's love and salvation. God has placed each of us exactly where we are. He designed us individually and strategically planted us in our time and location because He knows the difference we can make.

Esther was just an average girl. But God crowned her queen and used her to prevent the genocide of her people. Esther's cousin Mordecai warned her about Haman's hatred of the Jewish people and his plot to massacre them. He begged Esther to intervene with the king, but she hesitated at the risk—going before the king without being summoned could mean her death. So Mordecai offered a final warning: "Do not think that because you are in the king's house you alone of all the Jews will escape. For if you remain silent at this time, relief and deliverance for the Jews will arise from another place, but you and your father's family will perish. And who knows but that you have come to your royal position for such a time as this?" (Esther 4:13–14).

God put Esther exactly where she needed to be to prevent the annihilation of her people. And He has positioned you for maximum effect too. Do you see them? Don't be indifferent in their time of need.

The Wrong Crowd

Be happy when you are insulted for being a Christian,
for then the glorious Spirit of God rests upon you.
1 PETER 4:14 NLT

Jesus was coming to eat with him! Matthew could have skipped home. While his occupation had brought him great wealth, he was lonely. Called a traitor for collecting Roman taxes from his fellow Jews, Matthew was accustomed to rejection. But Jesus hadn't judged him for his reputation or his occupation. Jesus had simply said, "Follow me." The tax collector realized that he wanted to find out what made this man so different.

Matthew grinned as his raucous group of friends joined the party, but then some latecomers drew his gaze. He cringed inwardly as a group of Pharisees and scribes marched into his feast.

The Pharisee's brow arched toward his hairline as he scanned the gathering. "Why is Jesus eating with these sinners?" he asked.

Matthew's heart drummed a staccato rhythm in his chest. Would Jesus condemn him now in front of these condescendingly righteous leaders?

Jesus glanced at his dinner companions and smiled. "It is not the healthy who need a doctor, but the sick. I have not come to call the righteous, but sinners" (Mark 2:17).

Jesus knew that He was needed most by those trapped hopelessly in sin—the undesirables, the forgotten, the wretched. He found them where they were, as they were. And they were drawn to His open love for them. He cared about their problems and didn't browbeat them with their mistakes. He offered them hope even in their appalling state.

How often do we befriend only those who are like us? Do we avoid people we think are scary or different from us? Jesus gave us a new example. He didn't care who was the most popular, the best, or the brightest. And He didn't worry about tarnishing his own reputation in order to minister to those who weren't quite squeaky clean. Follow Jesus—be more concerned with loving people than with merely appearing good.

Keeping Up with the Joneses

You have been raised with Christ, set your hearts on things above, where Christ is, seated at the right hand of God. Set your minds on things above, not on earthly things. For you died, and your life is now hidden with Christ in God.

COLOSSIANS 3:1–3

Kathlynn scowled out her window. The neighbors were adding on to their house. . .again. Now her four- thousand-square-foot mansion was going to appear positively shabby next to the *palace* they were constructing. She sat down to consider her finances, biting her nails and eyeing the materials being hauled into her neighbor's gargantuan home.

Money was a lot tighter since her husband had lost his high-paying executive job. But somehow they had to keep their neighbors from discovering their financial distress. What would they think if they knew she'd had to give up her Louis Vuitton handbags? Her vacation home in the Caribbean? They'd say it was unfortunate. But she'd be snubbed.

We all long for something to fill the gaping void within us. We often think that accumulating stuff will bring us status, security, and confidence. But Jesus knew that material wealth could become a stumbling block of titanic proportions and that God alone could provide what we craved.

A rich young man once asked Jesus what he needed to do to obtain eternal life. Much to the man's disappointment Jesus replied, "If you wish to be complete, go and sell your possessions and give to the poor, and you will have treasure in heaven; and come, follow Me" (Matthew 19:21 NASB). Jesus had put his finger on the one thing the young man wouldn't sacrifice, even for heavenly treasure.

What are you holding on to—money, control, image, status? Jesus knew what gripped the rich young man's heart, just as He knows what we cling to. Are you trusting in God or something else? It is impossible to serve two masters, and we can't love God fully when we've given our hearts to fleeting pleasures. So surrender what you prize most to God, who is faithful to provide everything you need, in this life and for eternity.

Give Love Away

Give thanks to the God of heaven,
for his steadfast love endures forever.
PSALM 136:26 ESV

"Jesus loves me this I know." We often relegate this song to children's church, but its message is equally relevant to adults. Marinate in the truth of this familiar tune for a moment. Some people have only head knowledge of God's love, and others believe that they've already messed up so badly that God couldn't love them. But His love isn't conditional to our good behavior. "God shows his love for us in that while we were yet sinners, Christ died for us" (Romans 5:8 RSV). It's a huge comfort to know that Jesus loves us even with our flaws.

But do we understand what it means to be loved by a holy God? God is not aloof. He doesn't show His affection from a distance. "For the LORD your God is living among you. He is a mighty savior. He will take delight in you with gladness. With his love, he will calm all your fears. He will rejoice over you with joyful songs" (Zephaniah 3:17 NLT). Our mental image of God might be that of a stern and dignified deity, but this verse assures us of His feelings toward us. Not only is God with us, but He also delights and sings over us!

So what are we to do when we're bursting with God's love for us? Give it away! Scottish evangelist Henry Drummond said, "God is love. Therefore love. Without distinction, without calculation, without procrastination, love." We should love because God loves us. The apostle John echoed this sentiment: "Dear friends, let us love one another, for love comes from God. Everyone who loves has been born of God and knows God. Whoever does not love does not know God, because God is love" (1 John 4:7–8).

Does God's love permeate your thinking and direct your actions? Does your life confirm that you know God?

That's Not Fair

"The last will be first, and the first will be last."
MATTHEW 20:16

❖

"Life's not fair." Surely we all heard these words from our parents a few times growing up. And thankfully God isn't fair either—He's merciful.

In Matthew 20 Jesus tells the story of some whiny vineyard workers. The owner of the fields had hired help throughout the day. He hired some early in the morning, some in the afternoon, and some just before quitting time. And he had the audacity to pay them all the same amount!

Inevitably, the morning workers started complaining about how unfair it was that they had toiled all day in the scorching sun for the same wages as those who had worked for only one hour. One hour!

But the owner of the vineyard replied, "Don't I have the right to do what I want with my own money? Or are you envious because I am generous?" (Matthew 20:15).

Jesus made it clear that entrance into heaven and the salvation of our souls can be obtained in only one way—through the grace of God. We can't work long enough or hard enough to earn the righteousness He imparts to us through the blood of Christ. And He chooses to give everyone who accepts His offer the same reward. Whether we believe in Christ in our last hour on earth or we've spent our entire lives walking with God, our salvation is secure.

We shouldn't resent those who ran after their own pleasure every day for seventy years and then accepted God's grace at the end. They've likely lived with regrets and consequences for decades. Fortunately our heavenly Father is as benevolent as that vineyard owner. Because none of us deserves eternal life.

Have you ever been jealous of someone who lived it up and then made a deathbed confession of faith? Focus instead on the grace—the undeserved favor—and blessings that God has bestowed on you. Praise God for His generous mercy.

The Big Picture

"I will make all your enemies turn their backs and run. . . .
But I will not drive them out in a single year."
EXODUS 23:27, 29

A re we there yet?" The shrill wail floats to your ears from the backseat for the hundred and first time since you left home—twenty minutes ago. You grip the wheel a little tighter. It's going to be a long three-hour drive with an antsy five-year-old child.

Patience is tough. Ask any kid. But God doesn't usually work on our time schedules because we lack the proper perspective while He can see all the hidden repercussions for rushing His timetable. And in His wisdom and love, He waits patiently for us to mature into His plans. God promised the Israelites victory over their enemies, but there was just one tiny catch. They'd have to be patient. He wasn't going to give them instant success—for their own good! He knew they couldn't yet fill the land He'd promised them. And that would lead to problems: "the land would become desolate and the wild animals too numerous for you" (Exodus 23:29). God was looking out for them even when they were probably eager to settle down in their new zip code.

But don't confuse waiting with wasting time. Just as the Israelites had to be obedient and persistent in the meantime, we are to "draw near to God, and he will draw near to [us]" (James 4:8 NRSV). The first condition of this promise requires action on our part. We step closer to God by surrendering our lives to His will and studying His Word, and then He steps closer to us.

When the time was right, God went before the Israelites and gave them the land He'd promised. Sometimes we think that God is taking too long, and we're itching with impatience, but we have to choose to trust that our heavenly Father is taking care of all the details. "Those who wait for the LORD shall renew their strength, they shall mount up with wings like eagles" (Isaiah 40:31 NRSV).

No Prewash Needed

*But God showed his great love for us by sending Christ
to die for us while we were still sinners.*
Romans 5:8 nlt

━━◆━━━━━━◆━━◆━◆━━━━━◆━

Are you bothered by the dichotomy of rinsing the dishes before you load them in the dishwasher— whose supposed job is to *clean* the dishes? Well, lucky for us, God doesn't require a rinse cycle to make us fit for His love. "You see, at just the right time, when we were still powerless, Christ died for the ungodly. . . . But God demonstrates his own love for us in this: While we were still sinners, Christ died for us" (Romans 5:6, 8).

"While we were still sinners"—what amazing and comforting words those are to hear. God didn't send His Son to die for us because we were good enough to deserve it; He did it because He loved us. "This is how God showed his love among us: He sent his one and only Son into the world that we might live through him. This is love: not that we loved God, but that he loved us and sent his Son as an atoning sacrifice for our sins" (1 John 4:9–10).

We are helpless to save ourselves. We needed someone to rescue us: enter Christ. "For God so loved the world that he gave his one and only Son, that whoever believes in him shall not perish but have eternal life. For God did not send his Son into the world to condemn the world, but to save the world through him" (John 3:16–17).

Often we're tempted to try and clean ourselves up before coming to Christ. Some people even subscribe to the lie that the roof would collapse if they were to enter a church. But the truth is Jesus already knows who we are and every awful thought and misdeed we've ever committed—and He still died for us anyway. The next time you're tempted to doubt whether God cares about you, remember that He loved you even before you followed Him.

The Price of Peace

[Christ] will be our peace.
MICAH 5:5

How much would you pay for peace of mind? Insurance companies are forever playing on our insecurities and fears. Unfortunately we can't purchase real peace, although the world tries hard to sell us its version of tranquility. From yoga to retirement plans, there's no shortage of those hawking the latest fads in security.

But don't despair! The good news is that Jesus offers us a different kind of peace. "Peace I leave with you; my peace I give you. I do not give to you as the world gives. Do not let your hearts be troubled and do not be afraid" (John 14:27). Christ doesn't offer us a repackaged edition of this world's fleeting serenity, He extends lasting peace and comfort. Second Thessalonians promises "the Lord of peace himself give you his peace at all times and in every situation" (2 Thessalonians 3:16 NLT). We can rest in the knowledge that God is in control and be confident of God's provision in our every circumstance.

God's peace comes only through Christ—and it's free for us! No expensive premiums required. We can't buy it or find it within ourselves. Christ has already purchased our peace. "He was pierced for our transgressions, he was crushed for our iniquities; the punishment that brought us peace was on him, and by his wounds we are healed" (Isaiah 53:5). Jesus allowed Himself to be crushed so that we wouldn't have to be, and our peace comes from knowing that the price for our sins is covered. "God made him who had no sin to be sin for us, so that in him we might become the righteousness of God" (2 Corinthians 5:21).

Because of Jesus' sacrifice, we don't have to fear the present or the future. Our eternal destination is secure. So relax. Take a deep breath amid the frenzy and "let the peace of Christ rule in your hearts" (Colossians 3:15), because "the mind governed by the Spirit is life and peace" (Romans 8:6).

Busybodies Anonymous

A gossip goes around telling secrets,
but those who are trustworthy can keep a confidence.
PROVERBS 11:13 NLT

Oh, she must have something really good today, Janice thought. Cynthia was headed her way, and the gleam in her eye announced her intent. Janice rubbed her palms together and slid discreetly toward an empty Sunday school room. Cynthia slipped in behind her. "So." Cynthia quirked an eyebrow, milking the drama from the moment. "Did you hear about the Jordans?"

Gossip holds a tantalizing appeal that's hard to resist. When we have inside information it can be difficult to hold our silence. But gossip often stems from malicious lies spread out of anger or jealousy. It's a dangerous web to be enmeshed in. The apostle Paul warned, "Do not let any unwholesome talk come out of your mouths, but only what is helpful for building others up" (Ephesians 4:29).

While spreading rumors may seem harmless, it's not. And the Bible has some strong words to describe the effect of gossip: "Telling lies about others is as harmful as hitting them with an ax, wounding them with a sword, or shooting them with a sharp arrow" (Proverbs 25:18 NLT). Those are some pretty serious injuries! I guess the popular ditty "sticks and stones may break my bones, but words will never hurt me" doesn't exactly hold true. Verbal abuse *does* hurt.

Paul offers a practical solution to gossipers: "We hear that some of you are living idle lives, refusing to work and meddling in other people's business. We command such people and urge them in the name of the Lord Jesus Christ to settle down and work" (2 Thessalonians 3:11–12 NLT). Idleness leads to boredom, which can tempt us to stick our noses where they don't belong. So if you have too much time, find a way to serve God and get busy!

And remember what's supposed to be on our minds: "Whatever is true, whatever is noble, whatever is right, whatever is pure, whatever is lovely, whatever is admirable—if anything is excellent or praiseworthy" (Philippians 4:8).

Put on Kindness

But the fruit of the Spirit is. . .kindness.
GALATIANS 5:22

Do you relate to God as your heavenly Father or as a distant Lord? Often we focus on God's judgment and see Him as a detached and stoic deity who has little concern for us. We have a lot in common with the Israelites who "did not remember [God's] many kindnesses" (Psalm 106:7).

But kindness is a fruit of the Spirit—it's one of God's characteristics. And that means God is kind! Hosea 11:1, 4 says, "When Israel was a child, I loved him. . . . I led them with cords of human kindness, with ties of love. To them I was like one who lifts a little child to the cheek, and I bent down to feed them." God is our Father, and He cares tenderly for us just as we do our little ones.

God isn't disengaged from His creation. He provides for us. "He has shown kindness by giving you rain from heaven and crops in their seasons; he provides you with plenty of food and fills your hearts with joy" (Acts 14:17). Just as a mother feeds her children but also provides love and comfort, God also tends both our physical and emotional needs.

Jesus has a soft spot for children, and His tender kindness shines when He beckons them closer. " 'Let the little children come to me, and do not hinder them, for the kingdom of heaven belongs to such as these' " (Matthew 19:14). But Jesus' ultimate act of kindness came later—when He died for us. "When God our Savior revealed his kindness and love, he saved us. . . . He washed away our sins. . . . Because of his grace he declared us righteous and gave us confidence that we will inherit eternal life" (Titus 3:4–7 NLT).

Can you see God's kindness to you? Praise Him for His tender care. Jesus showed us kindness, so let's follow His example. Before you leave home "as God's chosen people, holy and dearly loved, clothe yourselves with. . .kindness" (Colossians 3:12).

Besieged

*I consider that our present sufferings are not worth
comparing with the glory that will be revealed in us.*
ROMANS 8:18

Mom, it's raining downstairs!" A broken water pipe has flooded your house.
Your kids are whining for dinner, but you've turned off the water main to
staunch the deluge. Your mom calls to say that your dad isn't doing well and has
to stay overnight at the hospital for observation. You have a big project due at
work tomorrow, and your husband has to go out of town and needs his clothes
washed. You're moving to a new house in one week, and Thanksgiving is two days
after that. Oh yeah, and you're seven months pregnant.

Besieged—ever felt this way? *Merriam-Webster* says to besiege is "to surround
with armed forces; to press with requests; to cause worry or distress to." It's a
feeling most women can relate to as they struggle to be a wife/mom/daughter/
career woman/cook/housekeeper. . .well, you get the idea. It seems that women
are forever destined to wear too many hats.

One evening Jesus' disciples were with Him in a boat. They were terrified
when "a furious squall came up, and the waves broke over the boat, so that it
was nearly swamped" (Mark 4:37). But amid this churning chaos "Jesus was in
the stern, sleeping on a cushion" (Mark 4:38). Surrounded by screaming men
and impending death, Jesus was peacefully snoozing. When His disciples frantically woke Him, He asked, "Why are you so afraid? Do you still have no faith?"
(Mark 4:40).

Where is our faith when the storms of life rage around us? Do we quake with
fear and discard our trust in God's faithfulness, goodness, and power to command
the swelling waves around us to "be still!" (Mark 4:39) as the disciples did?

Jesus said, "Come to me, all you who are weary and burdened, and I will give
you rest" (Matthew 11:28). When life boils around you and you're besieged, have
faith. Go to Jesus and refresh yourself in the peace and rest only He can provide.

Childlike

"Truly I tell you, unless you change and become like little children,
you will never enter the kingdom of heaven."
MATTHEW 18:3

M y dad is tougher than your dad. He can do anything!" When we're kids, our dads seem invincible. There is no job too hard for them, nothing they can't fix, and no question they can't answer. We trust them completely to keep us safe. We rest in the security of their love. And we never worry about whether they can provide for us.

As we grow older, we come to realize that our earthly fathers are only human. Some of the superhero shine tarnishes as we start to recognize their limitations. Sadly, our faith in our heavenly Father's abilities often follows the same jaded course.

But we're missing one vital fact. God is not human—He's the Master and Creator of the universe. And He never wants us to lose our wonder at His power. The prophet Jeremiah proclaimed, "O Sovereign LORD! You made the heavens and earth by your strong hand and powerful arm. Nothing is too hard for you!" (Jeremiah 32:17 NLT).

God promises that He has good plans for us. Just as we cheer on our children and desire wonderful achievements for their future, God says, "For I know the plans I have for you. . .plans to prosper you and not to harm you, plans to give you hope and a future" (Jeremiah 29:11).

Sometimes we evaluate God by our own limited standards—and our faith falters. As parents we might mess up royally. We may fail our children. But God never fumbles. He promises that "if you, then, though you are evil, know how to give good gifts to your children, how much more will your Father in heaven give good gifts to those who ask him!" (Matthew 7:11).

Reclaim your childlike faith. Rest in the assurance that nothing is too hard for our mighty Father who "makes [us] lie down in green pastures, he leads [us] beside quiet waters" (Psalm 23:2).

Stay Charged

We preach Christ crucified: a stumbling block to Jews and foolishness to Gentiles, but to those whom God has called, both Jews and Greeks, Christ the power of God and the wisdom of God.

1 CORINTHIANS 1:23–24

Blackout. The lights flicker and blink out. The refrigerator motor rumbles to a standstill. Silence permeates the darkness. Your power is gone. Sometimes we've simply overloaded a breaker, or maybe a fallen tree has short circuited the local electrical lines. Either way, it's a huge inconvenience to suddenly run out of power. All of our modern appliances are useless when they're cut off from the flow of electricity.

Who is your power source? Our batteries quickly run out of juice when we try to rely on our own strength. But when we accept Christ's gift of salvation we are able to connect to the power source of our faith: "You, though a wild olive shoot, have been grafted in among the others and now share in the nourishing sap from the olive root" (Romans 11:17).

When we're not plugged into God's Word, we're simply ineffective at walking in His ways. Without it we're reduced to stumbling around in the dark: "Your word is a lamp for my feet, a light on my path" (Psalm 119:105). God gave us the Bible to teach us how to live our new lives in Him. "For you have been born again, not of perishable seed, but of imperishable, through the living and enduring word of God" (1 Peter 1:23).

Jesus said, "I am the vine; you are the branches. If you remain in me and I in you, you will bear much fruit; apart from me you can do nothing" (John 15:5). Spending time studying God's Word and praying are crucial to our faith. Sometimes mature believers get bored with the routine or just think they're too busy. But it takes no time to read one verse, and you can always pray wherever you are. Spend some time with Jesus. Stay connected to the power that never fails.

Rock

My salvation and my honor depend on God;
he is my mighty rock, my refuge.

PSALM 62:7

Superstorm Sandy barreled into the Northeast coastline in 2012. Even after a year, thousands of people were still not able to rebuild homes that had been swept away or severely damaged by the furious storm. Sandy impacted an estimated 650,000 structures.

Sometimes the circumstances we encounter in life can rage with what seems like hurricane-force winds. Our lives can be flooded with trials and tragedy. It's so easy to be swept away by hard times. Our faith might tremble. If our foundation isn't set into the Rock, our house might be ripped away and destroyed in the turmoil. But Jesus explained to His followers how to withstand the tempest: "Everyone who hears these words of mine and puts them into practice is like a wise man who built his house on the rock. The rain came down, the streams rose, and the winds blew and beat against that house; yet it did not fall, because it had its foundation on the rock" (Matthew 7:24–25).

God is the Rock upon which we should set our foundation. "Trust in the LORD with all your heart and lean not on your own understanding; in all your ways submit to him, and he will make your paths straight" (Proverbs 3:5–6). What are you leaning on? You might want to check that it's strong enough to support you for the long haul. Many things on earth seem pretty sturdy, but when the winds blow, even ancient, massive trees can be torn from their roots.

Lean on God. Sometimes trusting Him can be hard when you don't understand why terrible things are happening. But He is the heavenly Father who loves you. He will never fail because "the LORD himself, is the Rock eternal" (Isaiah 26:4). Sink your foundation deep into the Rock.

Control Freak

*"I am the LORD, who made all things, who alone stretched
out the heavens, who spread out the earth by myself."*
ISAIAH 44:24 ESV

Will all the bossy, micromanaging perfectionists please stand up! Maybe you recognize these traits in yourself, or perhaps you know someone who fits this M.O. Controlling people can be harsh on those around them. If you're a control freak, you recognize the driving need to orchestrate every detail so things come out exactly right. Or if you know someone who is allergic to the passenger seat, you are well acquainted with the theory that yes, there is only one *right* way.

Someone has to take care of the details, and being organized isn't bad, but sometimes we can go too far. We need to be aware of our tendencies and act as Jesus would in spite of our impulses. Colossians 3:12, 14 says, "Clothe yourselves with compassion, kindness, humility, gentleness and patience.... And over all these virtues put on love." Are we wearing any of these garments when we're focused more on making *things* perfect than we are with showing *people* love?

When we think something isn't being done quite to our expectations, it's oh so easy to criticize and hijack the leadership position. We say that if we want something done right we have to do it ourselves. But whose feelings are we trampling in the process? Are we wrestling control from God's hands?

We can't do God's job for Him. As much as our egos entice us to believe we can bend circumstances to our will, in truth our heavenly Father is the one who hands out strength. "Yours, LORD, is the kingdom; you are exalted as head over all. Wealth and honor come from you; you are the ruler of all things. In your hands are strength and power to exalt and give strength to all" (1 Chronicles 29:11–12). Remember that God spins the universe, not you. And keep your criticism in check. Instead put on kindness, humility, gentleness, patience, and love.

Identity Crisis

My old self has been crucified with Christ.
It is no longer I who live, but Christ lives in me.
GALATIANS 2:20 NLT

Musician. Teacher. Doctor. Mother. Wife. How do you identify yourself? Most of the time when we meet new people we explain ourselves in terms of what we do. And often we seek fulfillment through our accomplishments or other people. Does being a mother to your children define you? Does your job? Does Jesus?

What is the essence of who you are? The apostle Paul explained to the believers in Colossae, "You died, and your life is now hidden with Christ in God. When Christ, who is your life, appears, then you also will appear with him in glory" (Colossians 3:3–4). How often do we find our identity in something other than Christ? What is the first thing people think when they see you? Is it, "She loves Jesus"?

When we become Christians, our old selves are supposed to die. But we often try to resurrect our sinful habits and ways of thinking long after we've discovered the new life that Christ has given us. We continue to hang out at the graveside instead of embracing the new creation we are in Jesus.

When we're young, and sometimes not so young, we waste a lot of effort trying to discover ourselves. And we think we'll find acceptance and completion by fitting into tidy categories. But Paul says this isn't the way to wholeness: "Here there is no Gentile or Jew, circumcised or uncircumcised, barbarian, Scythian, slave or free, but Christ is all, and is in all" (Colossians 3:11). There's only Jesus. He is our new identity.

Christ has given us a new life, a transformed life. Drop those old, dead habits and enter the freedom of living Jesus. When people see you, let them see the character of Christ in you.

Tantrum

" 'How gladly would I treat you like my children and give you a pleasant land,
the most beautiful inheritance of any nation.' I thought you would
call me 'Father' and not turn away from following me."

JEREMIAH 3:19

N o, no, no!" Toddlerhood—the perpetual state of no. It's natural for little tykes to latch on to this word when it's the only one they hear. They want to explore, and at times their curiosity gets them into trouble. They don't understand the potentially dangerous situations they get themselves into and often have a royal fit when Mom says no.

We like to think we've put our toddler days behind us, but how often do we balk and pout when our heavenly Father corrects us? Do your actions resemble those of a tantrum-throwing two-year-old child when God doesn't give you the answer you want, or have you grown in maturity? "When I was a child, I talked like a child, I thought like a child, I reasoned like a child. When I became a man, I put the ways of childhood behind me" (1 Corinthians 13:11).

As an adult you have gained through experience the foresight to protect little ones from some damaging consequences—from burns to bee stings. Now imagine the incalculable wisdom and love of your heavenly Father. "How great is God—beyond our understanding! The number of his years is past finding out" (Job 36:26).

We often boast of our own acumen, but compared to God, our prescience is pitifully limited. We play at checkers while God is a chess master. He sees the *eternal* ramifications of every action. "And these are but the outer fringe of his works; how faint the whisper we hear of him! Who then can understand the thunder of his power?" (Job 26:14).

When you're confused or on the brink of anger with God, consider that "as the heavens are higher than the earth, so are my ways higher than your ways and my thoughts than your thoughts" (Isaiah 55:9). Be comforted by your heavenly Father's sweeping perspective. Trust.

The Greatest Position

"Whoever wants to become great among you must be your servant."
MATTHEW 20:26

The highest-paying job. The biggest house. The most toys. The newest fashions. We have arrived at the top. The world tells us these things equal success. And everyone is endlessly jockeying for a greater position. With an increase in prestige we garner recognition, and people around us make sure we get what we want, exactly when and how we want it.

Jesus' disciples once argued about which of them would be the greatest. But Jesus' end to their bickering didn't exactly promise diamonds and pearls. He brought a child, probably one who was a bit scrawny and bedraggled, and said, "Whoever welcomes this little child in my name welcomes me; and whoever welcomes me welcomes the one who sent me. For it is the one who is least among you all who is the greatest" (Luke 9:48). Jesus wasn't measuring success with their yardstick.

It's easy to get wrapped up in selfish desires and our own comfort. But Jesus had other ideas for how to get ahead in His kingdom. "Whoever wants to become great among you must be your servant, and whoever wants to be first must be slave of all. For even the Son of Man did not come to be served, but to serve" (Mark 10:43–45).

Jesus didn't come to earth to set Himself up as king and demand all the comforts His castle could offer. Instead He came as a humble servant and demonstrated that servanthood was the path to greatness in His kingdom.

Serving others can be a tough job because it means putting ourselves last; we take the lower position. Instead of concentrating on getting our own needs met, we sacrifice our ease to give someone what he or she needs.

Take your eyes off your problems and desires for a moment. Look around. Is there someone who needs rescue—a kind word or a little help? Let's go out and "serve one another humbly in love" (Galatians 5:13).

Stress Buster

*"Be careful, or your hearts will be
weighed down with. . .the anxieties of life."*
LUKE 21:34

Have you ever been stressed out? Felt overwhelmed? It seems no one can escape anxiety. And it's probably safe to say that Martha was a tangled mess of stress when Jesus came to visit. If you've ever had a dinner party you can relate. Martha scampered around making sure the food was scrumptious—and hoped they wouldn't run out. Then she scrambled to get the place settings on the table and dashed through the house to check that it was still clean.

After welcoming her guests, Martha returned to slaving in the kitchen, probably sending a few dirty looks in Mary's direction. In Martha's opinion there were just too many preparations to sit as Mary was doing. Finally her frustration boiled over and she complained to Jesus, "Lord, don't you care that my sister has left me to do the work by myself? Tell her to help me!" (Luke 10:40).

Having problems isn't really our issue when stress overtakes us. It's how we react. Martha got snappy with everyone around her—including Jesus! And she was no doubt expecting to have her emotions vindicated by Him. But Jesus didn't scold Mary for being idle. Instead He chided her sister: "Martha, Martha. . .you are worried and upset about many things, but few things are needed—or indeed only one. Mary has chosen what is better, and it will not be taken away from her" (Luke 10:41–42).

Jesus wasn't at all concerned with dinner. After all, He'd fed five thousand with two loaves and five fish. He was confident He could manage with whatever Martha was whipping up. He wanted to give them the "bread of life" instead.

How do you react to the stress in your life? Do you rage at circumstances that are out of your control and bellow impatiently at people? Or do you step back and sit at the feet of Jesus, knowing that He can provide?

Growing Pains

No discipline seems pleasant at the time, but painful.
Later on, however, it produces a harvest of righteousness and peace.
HEBREWS 12:11

Everyone has a few stories about the folly of their youth. "Oh, I remember the time I. . ." These tales are usually bookended with "then my parents grounded me for a month and made me volunteer at the retirement home." Maybe they were hoping some of that aged wisdom would rub off!

Human parents aren't perfect. But one thing is true. They discipline their children because they love them. It's painful for a parent to watch beloved children stray from what they've been taught. In addition to our earthly parents we also have a heavenly Father who loves and corrects us. " 'My son, do not make light of the Lord's discipline, and do not lose heart when he rebukes you, because the Lord disciplines the one he loves, and he chastens everyone he accepts as his son' " (Hebrews 12:5–6).

God's discipline proves that we are His children. It verifies His immeasurable love for us. If you sense that God is chastening you, don't be resentful. Instead rejoice that you are His child! Look for the lesson He's teaching. "Endure hardship as discipline; God is treating you as his children. . . . If you are not disciplined—and everyone undergoes discipline—then you are not legitimate, not true sons and daughters at all" (Hebrews 12:7–8).

Unlike our earthly parents, God doesn't make mistakes. He doesn't have sin to influence His teaching methods. His discipline is perfect and purely for our benefit. He never strikes out in anger or embarrassment over our actions. He corrects only in love. "God disciplines us for our good, in order that we may share in his holiness" (Hebrews 12:10).

God sees what we can become instead of what we are. Sometimes growing can be painful. But in the end we transform into beautiful reflections of our heavenly Father. Let's pray the apple doesn't fall far from the tree!

What's Mine Is Yours

For we are God's handiwork, created in Christ Jesus to do good works,
which God prepared in advance for us to do.
EPHESIANS 2:10

W hen we're married, we tend to take possession of our husbands' stuff—especially where the house is concerned—even if we don't always extend him the same offer. With a smile we jest, "What's mine is mine, and what's yours is mine."

God gives us many gifts—time, money, possessions, abilities—but everything we call our own ultimately belongs to Him. And He asks that we use those things to further His kingdom. Jesus told of a man leaving for a trip in Matthew 25. He gathered his servants and gave each one a different amount of gold according to his abilities. The first received five bags of gold, the second, two, and the last received one bag.

The first two servants immediately went out and doubled their investments, but the third servant was afraid of what would happen if he lost his master's money, so he buried it in the ground.

When the master returned he praised the productive servants and promised them even more responsibilities because of their faithful service. " 'Well done, good and faithful servant! You have been faithful with a few things; I will put you in charge of many things. Come and share your master's happiness' " (Matthew 25:21).

But the last servant brought back only the gold he had received. The master, angered by his laziness, took his gold and gave it to the servant with ten bags and cast the lazy servant out.

Our talents, time, and money don't belong to us. We are merely overseers of God's wealth. And He doesn't want to see us wasting or neglecting His resources. Being a Christian doesn't grant us license to lounge around waiting for Jesus to return so we can go to our eternal home. We are meant to be about our Father's business, just as Jesus was. There's kingdom work to be done, and God has given us everything we'll need. Go use it for His glory.

The Letter of the Law

"These people honor me with their lips,
but their hearts are far from me."
MATTHEW 15:8

Children are masterful at circumventing their parents' rules without actually disobeying the words that they said. "You can't go to that party with your boyfriend" is creatively interpreted as *Okay I'll just meet him there,* even when the intended meaning was "You are not going to that party. Period."

Unfortunately we don't outgrow this propensity to fulfill the minimum requirement of rules and laws instead of obeying their intent. Jesus taught His followers that God's laws have a deeper purpose than just keeping us from killing one another. "You have heard that our ancestors were told, 'You must not murder. If you commit murder, you are subject to judgment.' But I say, if you are even angry with someone, you are subject to judgment! If you call someone an idiot, you are in danger of being brought before the court. And if you curse someone, you are in danger of the fires of hell" (Matthew 5:21–22 NLT).

God's intent was that we control our anger so it doesn't lead us into sin. Our actions are merely the end result of the sin we've already committed in our thoughts. "After desire has conceived, it gives birth to sin" (James 1:15). Jesus directed us to love one another. He taught that love is the greatest commandment and all the others hinge upon it. For most people it's terribly easy to make it through life without murdering anyone, but do we always treat everyone in love and resist our inclination to lash out in anger? We should examine the reasons behind God's laws so we can follow both the letter *and* intent of His commandments.

Do you ever follow God's rules literally but ignore His meaning? Have you ever felt, as the Pharisees did, that you haven't *really* broken any commandments? If so, consider whether you have ever failed to treat others with love.

Who, Me?

"All authority in heaven and on earth has been given to me. Therefore go and make disciples of all nations, baptizing them in the name of the Father and of the Son and of the Holy Spirit, and teaching them to obey everything I have commanded you. And surely I am with you always, to the very end of the age."
MATTHEW 28:18–20

"Go and make disciples." Those final words of Jesus often strike fear into the hearts of many believers who think that the only way to fulfill Christ's commission is to abandon their homes and head for dangerous parts unknown. And while some of us may be called to foreign lands, God's mission for us is about more than our address. It's a calling—a calling to love Jesus.

Jesus wept over the city of Jerusalem because the people would not accept His message—the peace and rest He offered through grace. He knew, as the prophet Isaiah had said, that "in repentance and rest is your salvation, in quietness and trust is your strength, but you would have none of it" (Isaiah 30:15). He saw the pain of the multitudes who were separated from Him.

Jesus' last order to His disciples, and to all believers, was to follow His example—to love the suffering mass of humanity as He did. We no longer belong to our own selfish desires. We now live to love. Out of our great love for Christ, His transformation of our lives should spill out to those around us.

Do your neighbors, coworkers, or even your family members know that you love Jesus? Are you doing the work that He has given you? The apostle Paul said, "God chose me and called me by his marvelous grace. . .so that I would proclaim the Good News about Jesus to the Gentiles" (Galatians 1:15–16 NLT). God may not be asking you to go far from your front door, but He is calling you to labor for Him—multiply His kingdom.

Humble Pie

The LORD mocks the mockers but is gracious to the humble.
PROVERBS 3:34 NLT

As women it seems we can't resist comparing ourselves to one another. We measure our status by the square footage of our houses, the carats in our jewelry, the labels on our clothing, the job titles we hold, and even the accomplishments of our children. And don't forget the inches of our waistlines and the cost of our hairstyles. Our vanity is boundless. And we rival one another for first place in even the most trivial things.

Enthralled by our own importance, we don't notice the people who are crushed by our bloated egos. But this selfish ambition is the antithesis of the humility of Christ. "Though he was God, he did not think of equality with God as something to cling to. Instead, he gave up his divine privileges; he took the humble position of a slave and was born as a human being" (Philippians 2:6–7 NLT).

That's a pretty serious plunge in prestige! Jesus gave up His status as God in order to put our needs first. We needed a savior. So He became the "Lamb of God, who takes away the sin of the world" (John 1:29).

The apostle Paul urged us to follow Christ's lead: "Do nothing out of selfish ambition or vain conceit. Rather, in humility value others above yourselves, not looking to your own interests but each of you to the interests of the others" (Philippians 2:3–4). Humility doesn't mean we fashion ourselves into doormats or degrade ourselves intentionally. It means we put others and God first, ahead of our own selfish desires—and we give God the credit. We build others up instead of tearing them down to make ourselves feel better or to achieve our own goals. Humility is the quality of quiet respect we show to all people.

Jesus considered each of us worth saving—at great personal cost. Let's forget about boosting our own positions and focus on showing others their value.

The Most Excellent Way

The entire law is fulfilled in keeping this one command:
"Love your neighbor as yourself."
GALATIANS 5:14

The apostle Paul opens the famous "love" chapter of 1 Corinthians by promising to show us "the most excellent way." He lets us know quickly that we can work our fingers raw, but if we're not motivated by love, we're wasting our efforts. "If I gave everything I have to the poor and even sacrificed my body, I could boast about it; but if I didn't love others, I would have gained nothing" (1 Corinthians 13:3 NLT).

In our modern culture, we throw around the word *love* pretty casually. It's often confused with personal pleasure or lust. But the picture of love that Paul paints for us is not self-directed. Instead, love denies self and gives unconditionally without expecting anything in return. We can't live this God kind of love without Him. We need His help to put aside our own selfish aspirations and cravings so we can love as Christ did—with no thought for ourselves.

So what does this God-love look like? Paul didn't leave us wondering. He told us exactly how to recognize love: it's patient, kind, not envious, not boastful, not proud, honors others, not self-seeking, not easily angered, doesn't keep record of wrongs, doesn't delight in evil, rejoices with the truth, always protects, trusts, hopes, perseveres—love never fails (1 Corinthians 13:4–8). Wow! It's a pretty tough challenge to put that kind of behavior into practice. But the best thing about Paul's message is knowing that's exactly the kind of love God has for us.

While we won't achieve perfection here on earth, when we enter God's presence in heaven we will be made complete. "For now we see only a reflection as in a mirror; then we shall see face to face. Now I know in part; then I shall know fully" (1 Corinthians 13:12). Based on that expectation, let's shower others with the love we will share in heaven.

The Seventh Day

"Remember the Sabbath day by keeping it holy. Six days you shall labor and do all your work, but the seventh day is a sabbath to the LORD your God. On it you shall not do any work, neither you, nor your son or daughter, nor your male or female servant, nor your animals, nor any foreigner residing in your towns."

EXODUS 20:8–10

During the French Revolution, the new regime instituted a ten-day week in 1793 to abolish Sunday as a holy day and de-Christianize the calendar. They touted their new system as rational and scientific. But rejecting God's provisions for rest didn't work out so well. The people were soon exhausted. They found one day of rest in ten to be so burdensome that they celebrated the return to a seven-day week in 1806.

Scientific research has also linked some of our bodies' physical processes to a circaseptan (seven-day) rhythm. God created us, and He knows that we need rest. He set the example by resting Himself. "For in six days the LORD made the heavens and the earth, the sea, and all that is in them, but he rested on the seventh day. Therefore the LORD blessed the Sabbath day and made it holy" (Exodus 20:11). He surely wasn't physically tired, but He took a break. And He asks us to rest with Him.

Our heavenly Father also promises good things to those who follow His instructions for some regular R&R. "If you keep your feet from breaking the Sabbath and from doing as you please on my holy day, if you call the Sabbath a delight and the LORD's holy day honorable, and if you honor it by not going your own way and not doing as you please or speaking idle words, then you will find your joy in the LORD" (Isaiah 58:13–14).

Is Sunday your day to frantically catch up on chores? Remember that this day belongs to God. And we will reap the benefits if we use it as He intends—to worship and rest.

Fixer-Upper

And we all, who with unveiled faces contemplate the Lord's glory,
are being transformed into his image with ever-increasing glory,
which comes from the Lord, who is the Spirit.

2 CORINTHIANS 3:18

House flipping is becoming an increasingly popular occupation with the recent real estate market crash. To most people these tired homes look like they have nothing left to offer. They see outdated dumps that should be torn down. But others look at these eyesores and see potential instead of problems. And many entrepreneurs are buying run-down houses, giving them a much-needed face-lift, and reselling them for a profit. Transformed from gross to gorgeous, they're changed from dysfunctional, hollow shells to warm homes filled with families.

God wants to transform our dysfunction just as flippers bring new life back into dilapidated structures. After you became a Christian, did your thoughts and actions change? Do you look different from the world? You should! The apostle Paul cautioned believers, "Do not conform to the pattern of this world, but be transformed by the renewing of your mind" (Romans 12:2).

What does this transformation look like? Our heavenly Father knows that we're helpless to change ourselves. We fail time after time when we try to be good apart from God. "I do not understand what I do. For what I want to do I do not do, but what I hate I do" (Romans 7:15). We reap nothing but frustration by trying to live up to God's standards alone.

But don't fret. God sent help. "I will ask the Father, and he will give you another Helper, to be with you forever, even the Spirit of truth, whom the world cannot receive, because it neither sees him nor knows him. You know him, for he dwells with you and will be in you" (John 14:16–17 ESV). The power of the Holy Spirit can refurbish our hearts. "God's love has been poured out into our hearts through the Holy Spirit" (Romans 5:5). Have you allowed the Holy Spirit to renew your mind?

Ever Ready

"Those who were ready went in with him to the marriage feast, and the door was locked. Later, when the other five bridesmaids returned, they stood outside, calling, 'Lord! Lord! Open the door for us!' But he called back, 'Believe me, I don't know you!' So you, too, must keep watch! For you do not know the day or hour of my return."

MATTHEW 25:10–13 NLT

During the American Revolutionary War, the Minutemen were the ultimate in rapid deployment. Always prepared, they were promoted as being "ready in a minute." As followers of Christ, we too are called to readiness.

No one knows the date of Jesus' return—although there's never a shortage of doomsday predictions. We speculate on everything from the Mayan calendar to a robot apocalypse. But not even Jesus knows when He'll be coming back: "But about that day or hour no one knows, not even the angels in heaven, nor the Son, but only the Father" (Matthew 24:36).

Jesus warns us to be alert and ready for His return. Ten bridesmaids were waiting for the bridegroom to arrive so they could enter the wedding feast. Five of them foolishly neglected to bring extra oil for their lamps, but the rest came prepared. The bridesmaids waited so long that they fell asleep. When the bridegroom showed up, half of them rushed out to meet him with their lamps glowing warmly while the others dashed out to buy more oil, causing them to miss out on the celebration.

Have you accepted Jesus as your Lord and Savior? He died on the cross for you and offers the forgiveness of sins and eternal life with Him. All you have to do is ask. "If you confess with your mouth that Jesus is Lord and believe in your heart that God raised him from the dead, you will be saved" (Romans 10:9 NLT). If you aren't ready, don't wait.

We aren't guaranteed tomorrow. No one knows how much time they have to live. Don't be late and miss the feast.

Unstoppable

If God is for us, who can be against us?

ROMANS 8:31

Woody Allen once said, "If you want to make God laugh, tell him about your plans." Often we make plans without consulting God, so it shouldn't come as a surprise when they don't line up with His designs for our lives or jobs or homes. How many times do we spend countless hours scheming and often even praying about the plans we're laying. We pray for a specific solution based on our goals. But sometimes things just don't turn out the way we're hoping they will. Sometimes there is no solution. Sometimes we face disappointment. Sometimes we fail.

But it's only in the aftermath of these letdowns that we can grow to trust God more. Because following our seeming defeats, we learn to search out God's best for us. And "if God is for us, who can be against us?"

This verse doesn't mean that we will never fail. It doesn't mean that we will never struggle or experience loss. And it most definitely does not mean that we will accomplish any harebrained idea that settles into our minds. It means that when we are following Christ and working toward His glory, nothing can get in the way of God's plans.

When you aren't achieving the outcome you'd hoped for, remember this promise: "If God is for us." Your heavenly Father has a good plan for you—one that will bring Him glory. " 'For I know the plans I have for you,' declares the LORD, 'plans to prosper you and not to harm you, plans to give you hope and a future' " (Jeremiah 29:11). But sometimes He has to redirect us toward His purpose. We're too easily distracted by our own desires.

If you are facing disappointment, don't lose heart. Exercise your trust in God. Remember that He loves you. He sees your situation, and He knows your deepest needs. He may solve your problem in surprising ways. Or He may lead you to something totally different—something you hadn't even thought to ask for.

Vision Check

"The eye is the lamp of the body. If your eyes are healthy, your whole body will be full of light. But if your eyes are unhealthy, your whole body will be full of darkness. If then the light within you is darkness, how great is that darkness!"
MATTHEW 6:22–23

When you started driver's training as a teenager, the instructor probably told you not to focus on the cars passing you in the opposite direction. If you look at the cars coming toward you instead of straight ahead at your own lane, your car will unintentionally drift toward the oncoming traffic. Our bodies tend to follow where our eyes are leading.

Jesus said that "the eye is the lamp of the body" (Matthew 6:22). Upon first glance this verse seems to be a little haphazardly stuck in between two well-known verses. Verse 21 says, "Where your treasure is, there your heart will be also." And verse 24 warns, "No one can serve two masters." But the common thread is focus. Where are your eyes looking? What treasures are you seeking? Are you serving God or self?

Many things can cloud our spiritual vision, making it hard for us to see the world from God's point of view. Often we're distracted by our own desires and goals. We work hard to gain what we want. And the things that we desire the most will control us. Are you focused on an eternal future in heaven or do you spend hours admiring and dreaming about things that won't last?

So how do we keep our eyes healthy so we can be filled with light? We keep our eyes fixed on God. Jesus said "I am the light of the world. Whoever follows me will never walk in darkness, but will have the light of life" (John 8:12). Jesus helps us maintain a true course.

Where are your eyes trained? Are they leading you into darkness? Be sure your godly vision is clear and focused. Stay to the light!

Beware the Weeds

"Still other seeds fell on fertile soil, and they produced a crop that was thirty, sixty, and even a hundred times as much as had been planted!"
MATTHEW 13:8 NLT

Every farmer knows the danger of weeds. Allowing weeds to flourish in their fields will seriously decrease their crop yields. Some weeds aren't overly aggressive and blend in with the plants, making them hard to spot. But other weeds are invasive and devastatingly destructive. They grow rapidly and compete with the other plants for nutrients, sunshine, and space. If left unchecked, they can overrun a garden, weakening or even killing the crops.

In Matthew 13 Jesus taught about a farmer planting his field. Some seeds landed on the path and were eaten by birds. Some of them landed on the hard, rocky ground and wilted in the sun because their roots were shallow. Some of them sprouted but were choked out by damaging weeds. But some of the seeds fell in the rich, black soil and grew into beautiful, bountiful crops.

The things we allow to take root in our lives affect us. Whether it is the thoughts we entertain or the people we spend time with, some influences can be as toxic as the strangling weeds in Jesus' parable while others can encourage and nourish us. The apostle Paul advised that "whatever is noble, whatever is right, whatever is pure, whatever is lovely, whatever is admirable—if anything is excellent or praiseworthy—think about such things" (Philippians 4:8). Our spiritual growth requires a healthy environment.

Do your thoughts and relationships strengthen or weaken your Christian walk? Unfortunately our surroundings tend to rub off on us. The more time we spend with good people thinking about wholesome things, the less likely that ugly weeds of temptation will stifle our growth. Just as some weeds are difficult to spot because they closely resemble the good plants, Satan is sneaky. Sometimes we allow one "small" sin into our lives, but it can multiply quickly. Surround yourself with godly, positive influences.

Learn to Listen

A truly wise person uses few words.
PROVERBS 17:27 NLT

Chatty Cathy. Gabby. Windy. Loose-lipped. The woman who prattles on and on and on is a popular—and sometimes accurate—stereotype. While all women aren't prone to incessant talking, many of us do enjoy a good chat over the phone or coffee with our friends, moms, or sisters.

But in our rush to share, sometimes we forget that communication is a two-way street. It involves listening as well as talking. How many times have you struggled to remember what someone told you because you were either talking or anticipating what you were going to say next?

If our conversation is a little light on the listening, it's impossible to convey genuine concern for the opinions and needs of others. We're not showing those we talk to that we value them. Our egocentric mind-set makes us insensitive to others who might need encouragement or advice.

The book of James has a fresh take on how we should interact with one another. "Be quick to listen, slow to speak" (James 1:19). When we remove the focus from ourselves, we're free to truly hear what others are telling us. At times we spout off our opinions without pausing to consider whether we're speaking truth and wisdom.

Jesus said, "Everyone will have to give account on the day of judgment for every empty word they have spoken" (Matthew 12:36). That isn't really a verse that most of us want to hear. We've all participated in our share of idle chatter. But we can make a new commitment to listen more and carefully consider our words.

Are your listening skills a little rusty? Next time you're in a conversation, pay attention to whether you spend more time talking or listening. Make a conscious effort not to cut off the other person before he or she finishes talking. A little silence will give you time to choose your words wisely and shows you actually care what others have to say.

The Heart of the Matter

"I the LORD search the heart and examine the mind."
JEREMIAH 17:10

Our society is driven by image. Women especially are plagued with body-image insecurities. We're too tall, too short, our noses are crooked or long; we're too round, too straight. And the air-brushed models on TV and billboards only serve to perpetuate the unattainable ideal of modern beauty.

Imperfections aside, we still put great effort into making a stellar first impression. We spend a little too much on our dresses; cover our "flaws" with makeup; and pluck, scrub, and coif ourselves into the best possible version we can be. Even though we hand out the sage advice "don't judge a book by its cover," we all too often evaluate others based on outward appearances.

But God isn't fooled by the pretty masks we wear for one another. He looks deeper. "The LORD does not look at the things people look at. People look at the outward appearance, but the LORD looks at the heart" (1 Samuel 16:7). If we spent as much time cleaning up our hearts as we do grooming our bodies, we would really start looking more like Christ. "My old self has been crucified with Christ. It is no longer I who live, but Christ lives in me" (Galatians 2:20 NLT).

Working out and taking care with your appearance aren't wrong, but if we're more concerned with our flat abs than with the condition of our hearts, we may want to examine our priorities. "Train yourself to be godly. For physical training is of some value, but godliness has value for all things, holding promise for both the present life and the life to come" (1 Timothy 4:7–8).

David has been called a man after God's own heart, and he prayed, "You have searched me, LORD, and you know me" (Psalm 139:1). God knows our motivations. He sees our hearts. Make your prayer today, as David's was, "Create in me a pure heart, O God, and renew a steadfast spirit within me" (Psalm 51:10).

Shortcut

Everyone who competes in the games goes into strict training. They do it to get a crown that will not last, but we do it to get a crown that will last forever.

1 CORINTHIANS 9:25

L*ate again,* Meredith thought. She castigated herself for not being more organized and better at managing her time. Why did this always happen to her? Her kids had purposely set her clock ahead ten minutes to force her into punctuality. But it hadn't helped. She wasn't going to make it to Bible study on time tonight either.

Meredith stomped on the brakes as she came to a turn-off she'd never taken before. *Hmm. This road goes straight over to Jackie's street,* she thought. This route would be much shorter, but her husband had mentioned that this road was not well maintained. Making a snap decision, she jerked her wheel around and sped down the shortcut. A few potholes later, Meredith jumped at a loud pop and felt the car pull toward the curb as her flat tire flopped around its rim.

Maybe you've been tempted to try a shortcut to save yourself some energy or bypass some difficult steps. If you believe infomercials, there's an easier, faster way to accomplish everything from chopping vegetables to learning a foreign language—in five simple steps! The problem with shortcuts is they usually don't work. And most of the time they end up taking longer.

Our spiritual growth is no different. Shortcuts to a relationship with God don't exist. Hebrews 6:11 says we are to "show this same diligence to the very end, so that what you hope for may be fully realized." Paul compares walking with God to an athlete training for the games. There is no easy button, only persistence, faith, practice, and hard work. So resist the urge to cut corners in your spiritual life. Time spent with your heavenly Father is never wasted.

Lasting Love

I am convinced that nothing can ever separate us from God's love. Neither death nor life, neither angels nor demons, neither our fears for today nor our worries about tomorrow—not even the powers of hell. . .nothing in all creation will ever be able to separate us from the love of God that is revealed in Christ Jesus our Lord.

Romans 8:38–39 nlt

H*ow did I get here?* Selling herself for money wasn't one of the bright dreams she'd embraced for her future. Abandoned by her father, with a mother struggling below the poverty level, and lost in her own depression, she'd tried to fill the gaping void in her soul with a plunging spiral of drugs and sex. But she was left feeling unloved—and worse, unlovable.

Her future seemed bleak. She was alone and entangled in a cycle of sin. Maybe we'd cross to the other side of the street if she were to pass by. Or maybe some of us identify with her lonely, unwanted existence. But this redeeming truth holds firm: *God loves her.*

Nobody is truly unlovable, because when people fail us, leave us, or hurt us, God's love endures. No matter how bad we think we've been or what terrible circumstances we're entrenched in, our Father in heaven looks on us in love.

Jesus welcomed the prostitute who poured perfume on His feet and washed them with her tears. As His follower, how do you convey God's love to those the world deems unlovable? Do you know someone who is alone? Someone who is struggling? How can you bring God's compassion to his or her doorstep?

We live in the wonderful reality that God's love is unconditional. He is always there for us. He comforts us in tragedy and holds us through our tears. He won't withhold His love regardless of what we do or what is done to us. And we can't earn His affection with our deeds. He offers it freely.

Do you know that God loves you? Believe it! Nothing can separate you from the love of God.

The Taming of the Tongue

The tongue of the wise commends knowledge,
but the mouths of fools pour out folly.
PROVERBS 15:2 ESV

Forest fires are a major concern in the Western United States during the dry summer months. The tiniest spark can erupt into a violent inferno that quickly engulfs thousands of acres, destroying homes and lives in the process. A fire's destruction is complete and irreversible. Beautiful woodlands are reduced to blowing ashes, and the damage can't be undone.

James 3 compares the injury our tongues can cause to a raging fire and warns that "it corrupts the whole body, sets the whole course of one's life on fire, and is itself set on fire by hell" (James 3:6). Satan can use our words to divide and conquer.

Our tongues can cause serious injuries. "It is a restless evil, full of deadly poison" (James 3:8). A few angry words can irreparably damage a friendship. We would do well to treat our tongues with the same caution we give a loaded gun. How often do we speak rashly and immediately wish we could snatch our words back? Our mouths can get us into trouble in many ways:

- Boasting. "Like clouds and wind without rain is one who boasts of gifts never given" (Proverbs 25:14). Empty words are useless to build God's kingdom.
- Flattery. "In the end, people appreciate honest criticism far more than flattery" (Proverbs 28:23 NLT). We're good at buttering people up with insincere words to get what we want.
- Lying. "The LORD detests lying lips, but he delights in people who are trustworthy" (Proverbs 12:22). Lies can damage both our relationships and our ministry for Christ.
- Babbling. "Too much talk leads to sin. Be sensible and keep your mouth shut" (Proverbs 10:19 NLT). Know when to stay silent.
- Arguing. "The Lord's servant must not be quarrelsome but must be kind to everyone" (2 Timothy 2:24). God desires unity among His children.

Guard your words carefully. Use them to encourage and draw people to Jesus.

Objects of Mercy

"Blessed are the merciful, for they will be shown mercy."
MATTHEW 5:7

Someone hurt you. How did you react? The world demands that we retaliate when we're injured. Get them back good so they'll never hurt you again. Revenge is sweet. Hit them where it hurts. Justice must prevail. Or is that vengeance?

We should be thankful that God doesn't play by our rules. Otherwise we'd all be doomed. Jesus revealed His Father's standard to His followers. "Be merciful, just as your Father is merciful" (Luke 6:36).

What exactly is mercy? *Merriam-Webster* defines *mercy* as "compassion or forbearance shown to an offender." *Forbearance* isn't a word we throw around much. It means "restraint in the face of provocation." Christ calls us to adopt an attitude of compassionate forbearance—we hold back our judgment, our paybacks, our anger, our pride—even when we've been wounded.

This is exactly the picture of God's mercy we find in Romans. "In the same way, even though God has the right to show his anger and his power, he is very patient with those on whom his anger falls, who are destined for destruction. He does this to make the riches of his glory shine even brighter on those to whom he shows mercy" (Romans 9:22–23 NLT). The NIV translation refers to us as "objects of his mercy" in verse 23.

What difference would it make in our attitudes and actions if we treated others as objects of our mercy? God could have wiped us from the face of the earth in His wrath—He has the right. But instead He rewards His children with a new life. "In his great mercy he has given us new birth into a living hope through the resurrection of Jesus Christ from the dead" (1 Peter 1:3).

Jesus told the Pharisees, "I desire mercy, not sacrifice" (Matthew 9:13). God wants so much more than empty religious rituals. He wants us to go out and demonstrate His mercy to the world. He longs for our passionate love and obedience.

The Practice of Prayer

*"But when you pray, go into your room, close the door
and pray to your Father, who is unseen. Then your Father,
who sees what is done in secret, will reward you."*

MATTHEW 6:6

❖・❖―❖・❖・❖―❖

How often do you talk with God? Do you have a regular running dialogue, or do you speak to Him only before meals or in church? God isn't looking for starched prayers. He wants our praise and humble, honest requests.

There are lots of methods for prayer. Some people like to write their prayers in journals because it helps them stay focused and gives them a record of God's movement in their lives. Some people take prayer walks to get away from the busyness of homes and jobs. It clears their minds of clutter so they can hear God. And others just chat with God as if they were talking to a friend.

Jesus offered His disciples a template for talking with their heavenly Father in Matthew 6. But He wasn't concerned with mere mimicry. Instead He showed them the basic elements to include in their conversations with God.

"Our father in heaven, hallowed be your name." Acknowledge who God is and remember his faithfulness to you.

"Your kingdom come, your will be done, on earth as it is in heaven." Surrender yourself to God's plan for your life. Listen—don't talk incessantly.

"Give us today our daily bread." Ask God for what you need—and for the needs of others. Be specific. God wants us to admit our needs to Him so He can be involved in our daily lives.

"Forgive us our debts, as we also have forgiven our debtors." Examine your life. What sins are you struggling with? Repent and ask God to forgive you. Don't hold grudges against people who have wronged you.

"Lead us not into temptation, but deliver us from the evil one." Ask God for strength to resist the devil's schemes. We pray because we desperately need God.

Develop a daily habit of prayer. Your heavenly Father is waiting to talk with you!

Who's Your Hero?

And you should imitate me, just as I imitate Christ. I am so glad...
that you are following the teachings I passed on to you.

1 Corinthians 11:1–2 nlt

Who do you emulate? The world is full of potential role models, some good, some less so. Do you yearn to look like the model or actress you admire or to be that organized mom who always seems to have everything just right—well-behaved kids, folded laundry, and everything in its place? There's nothing wrong with staying fit or caring for our kids and homes, but we sometimes overlook our most vital standard for living—Jesus.

A few years ago the popular phrase "What would Jesus do?" dominated Christian marketing. But familiar mottos can lose their effectiveness when we merely repeat the words without stopping to examine the truth they expose. How would our daily behavior alter if we asked ourselves this question before we acted? The apostle John wrote, "Those who say they live in God should live their lives as Jesus did" (1 John 2:6 nlt).

The catch? In order to walk in the WWJD? creed, we have to know the answer to the question—to follow Christ's example we must first know and love Him. Jesus summed things up nicely for the Pharisees when they asked Him which commandment was the greatest: " 'Love the Lord your God with all your heart and with all your soul and with all your mind.' This is the first and greatest commandment. And the second is like it: 'Love your neighbor as yourself.' All the Law and the Prophets hang on these two commandments" (Matthew 22:37–40).

It's pretty awesome to realize that the answer is so straightforward. What would Jesus do? Love. "This is my commandment, that you love one another as I have loved you" (John 15:12 esv). Let's make our new ambition to "walk in love, as Christ loved us and gave himself up for us" (Ephesians 5:2 esv).

Can You Take the Heat?

When you walk through the fire, you will not be burned;
the flames will not set you ablaze.

Isaiah 43:2

———•—•———•—•—•—•———•—•

King Nebuchadnezzar's mammoth statue of gold shimmered in the sun. His officials waited before the image of their sovereign in restive anticipation. The king had decreed that his people fall down and worship the image when the music played. But when the band began a sprightly tune, the crowd gasped—three Jewish captives remained standing.

Livid, the king ordered Shadrach, Meshach, and Abednego to be thrown into a furnace and burned alive if they continued their disobedience. But they replied, "The God we serve is able to deliver us....But even if he does not, we want you to know, Your Majesty, that we will not serve your gods" (Daniel 3:17–18).

God rewarded their refusal to compromise by saving them from the flames. When they strolled out of that furnace, they didn't even smell like smoke! And because of their faithful obedience to God, His power became known in Babylon and the Jewish captives were permitted to worship God.

We may not be threatened by literal fire for our faith, but do we stand up for God no matter what? Or do we follow the crowd by laughing at a crude joke or listening to gossip? If you take a stand for Jesus, you will stick out. And it can hurt. But just as Shadrach, Meshach, and Abednego would have killed their witness for God if they had bowed down to that golden image, we invalidate our message of Jesus' life-altering love when we prostrate ourselves at the feet of fear, jealousy, greed, or pride.

Don't compromise. Instead, remember that God is good and powerful. He calls us to stand with Him against the evil that saturates this world and spread His message of redemptive grace. You never know what victory God can work through our faithfulness to Him, because He achieves eternal results through our temporary trials.

Input/Output

Let the word of Christ dwell in you richly.
COLOSSIANS 3:16 ESV

"This workout program is a joke." The body gazing back at her from the full-length mirror hadn't changed much in the last four weeks. She had been doing all the routines for the prescribed amount of time, but the promised results hadn't materialized. She still looked twenty pounds overweight. In a flash of honesty she admitted that she hadn't exactly followed the diet plan. Mounds of yummy food at Thanksgiving had beckoned her—and it's not reasonable to refrain when everyone else is stuffing themselves, right? Then there were the morning doughnuts she couldn't give up. Oh, and that chocolate cake had whispered her name last night.

Are you dissatisfied with your spiritual results? Do you show up at church every Sunday, but fail to see any changes in your attitude or actions from Monday through Saturday? Maybe it's time to change your input. We've all heard the popular wisdom about becoming what we consume. What do you allow into your head and your heart on a daily basis? Where do your thoughts linger?

Just as exercise alone isn't enough to lose weight if you're still eating too many calories, sitting in a pew on Sunday morning isn't very effective if you're not feeding yourself the right spiritual food. Science is proving more and more the link between our diets and our health. And we can't expect to be spiritually healthy when we fill our minds with junk.

God advises that we "fix these words of mine in your hearts and minds; tie them as symbols on your hands and bind them on your foreheads. . . .Talking about them when you sit at home and when you walk along the road, when you lie down and when you get up. Write them on the doorframes of your houses and on your gates" (Deuteronomy 11:18–20). He wants us to constantly dwell on His teachings and promises. If you're looking for better results, try filling your mind with God's Word.

Feeling Frustrated?

For the happy heart, life is a continual feast.
PROVERBS 15:15 NLT

❖

You feel it building. Your chest constricts. Your teeth gnash together, and your respiration rate skyrockets. Adrenaline powers through your arteries. Your frustration is about to erupt like Mount Vesuvius and rain down fiery destruction on anyone who blocks your path.

Irritation—it often strikes when we don't get our way. Something or someone is preventing us from doing what we want, when and how we want. Welcome to life. We don't always get what we want; this fact holds true for both children and adults.

But our frustration doesn't really stem from the actions of others. We develop it internally. We choose how we react. Sure, we can charge others with causing our problems, but the choice is ours. When we can't seem to reach our goals or things aren't going our way, sometimes we have to learn to let go—release some of the control we're iron fisting. Micromanaging our lives can lead to some serious frustration.

We usually try to blame others for our emotional outbursts, but if you struggle regularly with irritation, look to yourself. Jesus recognized this human habit of avoiding self-examination. He asked, "Why do you look at the speck of sawdust in your brother's eye and pay no attention to the plank in your own eye?" (Matthew 7:3). Our reactions to problems and people are often more personally revealing than we're comfortable with.

Consider this: Do frustration and irritation improve your situation? Do they get you what you want? More importantly, does frustration glorify God? It's certainly not on the list of His Spirit's fruits. So why should we continue reacting this way?

"For freedom Christ has set us free. Stand firm therefore, and do not submit again to a yoke of slavery" (Galatians 5:1 NRSV). Jesus has freed us from our old behavior. So relax and definitely don't lose your temper over every little aggravation! Leave the control to the Master.

Follow Him

To this you were called, because Christ suffered for you,
leaving you an example, that you should follow in his steps.
1 Peter 2:21

Goals are great. They help us define what we want and how we're going to get there. They keep us from getting sidetracked by all the glittery distractions we encounter. Having a purpose gives us a standard by which to judge our actions. Have we reached for our goals today or wasted time on inconsequential diversions? Goals give us focus.

We often stress about finding God's will, especially when we're young. We say, "Father, I want to follow You. But where are we going?" We sometimes think that a single major decision, often a career, will set us on the path to God's plan for our entire lives, but if we mess this one up, we're doomed.

And we should seek God's opinion on major life choices: He cares about every detail. But thinking that God's will hinges on how we earn a living or what house we live in is a tad misguided. God "works out everything in conformity with the purpose of his will" (Ephesians 1:11). It all boils down to goals. God's objective in this world often isn't the same as ours. Our society is excessively materialistic, but the accumulation of wealth isn't one of God's priorities. Jesus said, "You cannot serve both God and money" (Luke 16:13).

So while we struggle for a bigger house and a shinier SUV, Jesus is calling, "Follow me, and I will make you fishers of men" (Matthew 4:19 ESV). Don't doubt that God attends to every aspect of our lives, but His purpose for us is to further His kingdom. "He is patient with you, not wanting anyone to perish, but everyone to come to repentance" (2 Peter 3:9). He is calling us to introduce others to the love of Jesus.

Do you really want to know God's will? Are you ready to surrender to His calling? His goals might not match yours. But the rewards far outweigh the cost.

Falling Walls

By faith the walls of Jericho fell,
after the army had marched around them for seven days.
HEBREWS 11:30

It looks unconquerable. The obstacle before us seems too big. Whether it's a fast-approaching deadline at work or what seems like an impossible situation at home, we just don't believe we have the strength, time, or resources to overcome.

When the Israelites crossed the Jordan River into the Promised Land, God led them smack into the massive, impregnable double walls around the stronghold of Jericho. They probably craned their necks and shielded their eyes with the flat of a hand just to get a look at the height of this fortress.

Not one but two walls surrounded the city. The inner wall sat atop an earthen embankment that sloped upward from an outer retaining wall. Its base towered forty-six feet above the ground outside the lower wall. The retaining wall alone was twelve to fifteen feet high and on top of that was a mud-brick wall reaching over twenty feet. Those are some impressive defenses!

But God didn't instruct the Israelites to start building ladders. Instead He said all they had to do was. . .march? And on the seventh day the priests blew their horns and the walls collapsed. God had promised Joshua beforehand, "See, I have delivered Jericho into your hands" (Joshua 6:2). The supposedly impenetrable defenses of Jericho were no match for God Almighty.

So why all the marching and trumpets? God wanted to remove all doubt about who brought Jericho down. The glory belongs to Him. But He also wanted the Israelites to show faith and willingness to follow His instructions. Their obedience brought victory.

What wall looms in front of you? When you face problems that you can't solve on your own, before you surrender to defeat remember that you aren't alone. God is with you. He walks beside you every day. If He can drop the walls of Jericho, He can help you through whatever seemingly insurmountable problem you face.

Unstained

Religion that is pure and undefiled before God,
the Father, is this. . .to keep oneself unstained from the world.
JAMES 1:27 ESV

Set apart. Not of this world. Different. How do we live holy lives? God calls His children to cast off the sin and evil of this world and to "be holy, because I am holy" (Leviticus 11:44). He isn't willing to share our affections. He wants our wholehearted, undivided love and worship.

The Old Testament Israelites are famous for their fickle faith. God delivered them from slavery in Egypt through miraculous plagues and defeated the Egyptian army with one crushing wave. And yet the minute they were safe, they convinced Aaron to fashion them an idol of gold. They abandoned their mighty God in order to bow before something that satisfied their senses.

We might find Leviticus a bit obsolete, but God's laws are never arbitrary. He wanted to protect the Israelites and distinguish them as His beloved children. Many of the animals He forbade were disease-carrying scavengers. Pigs were regularly sacrificed to pagan gods, and serpents symbolize sin.

God's rules are still meant to preserve us and set us apart. While we probably don't have a golden calf, our idols are possibly more insidious—money, our physical bodies, achievement, self-glorification. If we aren't serving God alone, we aren't living in holiness. "Do not love the world or anything in the world. If anyone loves the world, love for the Father is not in them. For everything in the world—the lust of the flesh, the lust of the eyes, and the pride of life—comes not from the Father but from the world" (1 John 2:15–16). When you're tempted to partake in something questionable, ask yourself, "Would I be ashamed if Jesus were here now?"

Jesus freed us from the deadly power of sin, and "we have been made holy through the sacrifice of the body of Jesus Christ once for all" (Hebrews 10:10). Search your heart for things you've put ahead of God. After all, what lasting benefits can they offer?

Who's Your Neighbor?

If you love those who love you, what reward will you get?
MATTHEW 5:46

H ere comes the rag lady." Amber snickered with her friends. Emily was a single mom who struggled to pay her bills. She lived in a bad neighborhood where the rent was low and wore secondhand clothes so she could provide for her son. But Amber's husband was a CEO, and they lived in an upper-class community. She never had to worry about money, and shopping was her favorite hobby. But she took every opportunity to mock Emily for her lack. She thought her entitled life put her above the problems of common people.

But Amber's rose-colored lenses were shattered when her son was diagnosed with leukemia. She was devastated, but her society friends withdrew from her as if the disease would somehow taint their immaculate lives.

Amber was surprised one afternoon when she answered the elegant chimes of their front door. Standing on her front step, her arms laden with a dinner prepared for Amber's family and offering to watch her other children during her son's numerous hospital visits was Emily. Tears stung Amber's eyes as she welcomed her inside.

Jesus told a similar version of this story featuring a helpful Samaritan. Jesus told us to love our neighbors. But often we try to put limits on who fits into the "neighbor" category. Are they people of similar financial status? The same race? Or perhaps only people who believe in Jesus? Exactly who are we supposed to show God's kindness to? Jesus' answer is simple: "Love your enemies, do good to those who hate you" (Luke 6:27). We aren't to discriminate when spreading kindness.

The Samaritan in Jesus' story was hated by the Jews, yet he stopped to help a Jew who had been assaulted by robbers even after the beaten man's fellow countrymen had passed him by, choosing not to get involved in the messy situation. Jesus' marching orders for His followers? "Go and do likewise" (Luke 10:37).

Are You Willing?

Then the LORD called Samuel. Samuel answered, "Here I am."

1 SAMUEL 3:4

❦

"Fine. I'll do it, but I won't like it." Kids often grumble when they're told to clean their rooms or take out the trash, but how often does this attitude of begrudging obedience creep into our Christian lives?

God doesn't target the strongest, the most skilled, or the most confident. In fact, many of His chosen ones seem downright ill-equipped for His mission. So why did He single them out? He picked them because they were willing to be instruments for His glory.

Speech was difficult for Moses, yet God sent him to speak to Pharaoh. Mary was an unmarried teenager and God chose her to raise His Son. The apostle Paul was murdering Christians with gusto until he saw the Light—literally—and was transformed into the radical first-century missionary who penned much of the New Testament. They don't seem like the obvious choices, but their response to God's call echoed Paul's: "Lord, what wilt thou have me to do?" (Acts 9:6 KJV).

God uses those who are available. We may feel woefully inadequate for whatever God has set before us. The apostle Paul struggled with his own "thorn." The Bible doesn't tell us exactly what plagued him, but whatever this debilitating problem was, God promised him, "My grace is sufficient for you, for my power is made perfect in weakness" (2 Corinthians 12:9). When we admit our weakness, our inability, we give the glory to God and recognize His strength. In spite of our weaknesses—even because of our weaknesses—God can work through us.

We often say that we are seeking God's will. But are those words just empty "Christianese"? Walking in God's purpose can be uncomfortable and demanding. It might mean sacrificing things we desire. It may require our time, money, and energy. But He's asking, "Come, follow me" (Matthew 4:19). The eternal rewards for following Jesus are well worth the wait. Is God nudging you to action? Is your heart willing?

Slave to Christ

You are not your own; you were bought at a price.
1 Corinthians 6:19–20

The English word *Christian* is derived from the Greek cristianos, which means "a person belonging to, one who is the property of, or a slave of Christ." As believers we literally name ourselves Christ's slaves, because out of His unsurpassed love for us Christ offered a steep purchase price to redeem us from death. The currency was blood—His blood.

It may prick our pride to be labeled slaves. We usually envision slaves as oppressed, exhausted forced laborers who have no hope of freedom. But this isn't the type of slavery that Jesus paid so dearly to offer us. Instead He promised, "Come to me, all of you who are weary and carry heavy burdens, and I will give you rest. Take my yoke upon you. Let me teach you, because I am humble and gentle at heart, and you will find rest for your souls. For my yoke is easy to bear, and the burden I give you is light" (Matthew 11:28–30 NLT).

The apostle Paul freely called himself "a slave of Christ Jesus" (Romans 1:1 NLT). The type of slave that Paul is referring to has no will of his own. He lives to fulfill his master's will until death. But unlike human masters, it is an honor to serve the Master and Creator of the Universe. Through Christ we are bound in a servanthood of love.

To live as obedient bond slaves of Christ, we must forsake all other masters and "throw off everything that hinders and the sin that so easily entangles" (Hebrews 12:1). Our willingness to obey Jesus makes us usable servants to Him. Have you abandoned your own will to freely wear the yoke of Christ?

The Power to Forgive

"But if you do not forgive others their sins,
your Father will not forgive your sins."
MATTHEW 6:15

Your sister died today." The words rang in Susan's head. She hadn't seen her sister in ten years. They'd quarreled a decade ago over their mother's cancer treatments. Angie hadn't thought the doctors were doing enough, and Susan had tried to carry out their mother's wishes. Now her sister was also gone, another victim to the same disease that had stolen their mom from them.

Susan's anger had mellowed over the years, but she'd been too stubborn and too entrenched in her habit of avoiding her sister. And now her chance at reconciliation was gone. She was swallowed by a yawning remorse. How had she sat in church every Sunday with this burden and not laid it down at Jesus' feet? Now she would never see Angie's sky-blue eyes or hear her ridiculous snorting laughter again in this life.

Missed opportunities can become our greatest regrets. Anger, pride, stubbornness, pain, and fear can prevent us from stretching out a hand of forgiveness to those who have hurt us. But Christ suffered the ultimate affront—mocking, beatings, and finally death. And yet He didn't lash out in anger or call down the wrath of His almighty Father. Instead, while they killed Him He prayed, "Father, forgive them, for they don't know what they are doing" (Luke 23:34 NLT).

As believers in Christ we are commanded to follow His example and forgive others. Peter once came to Jesus to inquire how many times he should forgive someone for wronging him. He offered what he surely thought was the magnanimous suggestion of seven times. But Jesus answered, "No, not seven times. . .but seventy times seven!" (Matthew 18:22 NLT).

Romans 3:23 reminds us, "For all have sinned and fall short of the glory of God." We are all flawed and wretched beings in need of God's mercy. So how can we offer anything less than unreserved forgiveness to one another?

Love in the Small Stuff

The only thing that counts is faith expressing itself through love.
GALATIANS 5:6

Have you ever wished for a billboard sign from God, maybe even one with glowing neon that screams, "Go This Way!"? Unfortunately, we often find ourselves scratching our heads about which way leads to God's plan. Sometimes we even randomly scan the scriptures hoping for divine inspiration to strike. Or we make deals with God in order to speed up His timing.

God has a specific plan for each of us, and following His plan requires faith, trust, patience, and obedience. We should take comfort in the knowledge that we serve a big God who has a much better perspective on our future than we do. But sometimes we get so caught up in worrying about the big decisions of life that we forget to follow Christ in the small stuff of everyday life.

When asked which commandment was the greatest, Jesus said, " 'Love the Lord your God with all your heart and with all your soul and with all your mind.' This is the first and greatest commandment. And the second is like it: 'Love your neighbor as yourself' " (Matthew 22:37–39). The thing He most desires of us is love—love for Him and love for one another.

How often do we snap at our spouses in impatience or criticize our friends. Many believers in Christ are suffering from a love deficiency. Paul says in Galatians 5:13, "You, my brothers and sisters, were called to be free. But do not use your freedom to indulge the flesh; rather, serve one another humbly in love."

The Bible is filled with God's laws. And it's true, we humans will never be able to follow all of them, but Jesus simplified everything for us by asking only that we love. "Love one another, for whoever loves others has fulfilled the law" (Romans 13:8). When we shift our focus from ourselves to concentrating on serving others in love, we can be sure we're walking God's path.

Get in Shape

Suffer hardship with me, as a good soldier of Christ Jesus.
2 TIMOTHY 2:3 NASB

Do you enjoy carbs a little more than you should? Do those Christmas cookies (or Valentine's Day or Easter or Halloween or, hey, isn't it Chocolate Cake Day?) seduce you with their sweet lies of satisfaction? We've all overindulged at some point, and after we've succumbed to that sugary temptation, we usually stumble off the scale in remorse. It still counts if we keep one toe on the ground, right?

Following our "holiday" excess, there's no lack of solutions for the war with our waistlines—or hips! Every January some of us roll out a new fad diet and a trendy exercise plan in hopes that we can starve and drip away those five extra pounds (okay ten!). Others opt to pop a pill or schedule some liposuction to make their skinny dreams come true.

While our society is viciously focused on the ideal weight and the perfect body shape, carrying around a little extra in the trunk does hurt our health and slow us down. While some may never categorize themselves as athletic, it's important to be physically fit. But there's also another often-neglected area that we need to train.

Are you spiritually fit? It's imperative that we stay in shape spiritually. The apostle Paul cautions: "Discipline yourselves, keep alert. Like a roaring lion your adversary the devil prowls around, looking for someone to devour. Resist him, steadfast in your faith" (1 Peter 5:8–9 NRSV). Don't give Satan the opportunity to pounce. Study God's Word, pray, and fellowship with other followers of Christ. Build your spiritual strength and "strip off every weight that slows us down, especially the sin that so easily trips us up. And let us run with endurance the race God has set before us" (Hebrews 12:1 NLT). Don't forget your spiritual workout today!

Don't Worry, Rejoice!

"I have told you this so that my joy may
be in you and that your joy may be complete."
JOHN 15:11

❦

Don't worry, be happy." Have you ever caught yourself offering the advice of this catchy, bouncing tune? It's a common misconception that believers in Christ are supposed to be happy all the time. And the apostle Paul did write a variation on this theme, but with one important distinction—joy. "Be full of joy in the Lord. I say it again—rejoice! . . . Don't worry about anything" (Philippians 4:4, 6 NLT).

The difference between joy and happiness is clearer if we examine their opposites. The opposite of happiness is depression while the opposite of joy is fear. Joy is a constant state of being, an inward peace and contentment. But happiness is a transient state determined by external events or feelings. So it makes sense that immediately after Paul encouraged the Philippian believers to rejoice, he then said not to worry.

Our emotions are volatile, reaching both the soaring heights of exhilaration and the black abyss of depression. But as followers of Christ we "are filled with an inexpressible and glorious joy, for you are receiving the end result of your faith, the salvation of your souls" (1 Peter 1:8–9). Through Christ, we have joy in spite of our circumstances, not because of them. Living in joy requires that we surrender our anxiety and fear and trust in God's goodness and power to use our circumstances for His purposes, to grow His kingdom. We must want God's plan more than we desire our own comfort and satisfaction.

God doesn't tell us not to worry because nothing bad will ever happen to us. He knows that "in this world you will have trouble. But take heart! I have overcome the world" (John 16:33). We rejoice because the victory is already ours!

Are anxiety, worry, fear, or lack of control keeping you from experiencing joy? Or can you echo Job's words: "Though he slay me, yet will I trust in him" (Job 13:15 KJV)?

God Is in the Details

He determines the number of the stars and calls them each by name.
Great is our Lord and mighty in power; his understanding has no limit.
PSALM 147:4–5

W ho doesn't love a good wedding? The flurry of activity, the cake, the dress, the invitations, the flowers, the kiss—they set our romantic hearts fluttering. But throughout the preparation and planning for our day of matrimonial bliss, we quickly discover that our grooms are simply not into details. We might entice them into a cake tasting with the promise of pastries, but china patterns and flower arrangements usually aren't their forte. And our frustration rises at their apparent lack of concern over every aspect of our long-dreamed-for day.

Thankfully we have a detail-oriented heavenly Father. He couldn't have created the complexity of our DNA or the intricate and balanced physical laws of the universe we live in if the smallest feature escaped His notice. There's no problem we can't bring to Him and no facet of our lives He isn't interested in. Matthew 10:30 promises that "even the very hairs of your head are all numbered."

Some people are afraid to "bother" God with the little problems and worries they have every day, but the apostle Peter recommended, "Cast *all* your anxiety on him because he cares for you" (1 Peter 5:7, emphasis added). He asks for all of our worries, not just the momentous, life-altering ones. We should seek God's heart in every aspect of our lives: He cares about us enough to notice each strand of hair.

Too often we try to solve our problems without involving God. We might ask a friend or consult the internet for information when our Creator and Counselor is only a prayer away. God set our world in motion, created each of us individually, and has all knowledge of the past, present, and future. Wouldn't we be wise to trust Him first?

Where do you go first when you need advice? Do you trust God to direct even the smallest details of your life?

Be a Living Sacrifice

In view of God's mercy, to offer your bodies as a living sacrifice,
holy and pleasing to God— this is your true and proper worship.

ROMANS 12:1

D eath can be gruesome. But God commanded the Old Testament Israelites to sacrifice animals to remind them of the weighty cost of sin. God created us for companionship; He walked in the garden with Adam and Eve. But sin gouged a chasm between God and His wayward children. In His mercy, God had a plan to restore that relationship. But first their sin had to be covered by innocent blood. Leviticus 1:9 says, "It is a burnt offering. . .an aroma pleasing to the LORD." God accepted their sacrifices because they reflected repentant, obedient hearts.

The Israelites were to offer only unblemished sacrifices as a symbol of God's holiness and to point the way to Jesus—the last and perfect Lamb. Because Jesus died in our place, we can now come freely to God. And sacrifice is a thing of the past. Or is it?

As believers in Christ, the apostle Paul calls us to a new way of sacrifice. He urges us to become living sacrifices to God if we want to truly please and worship Him.

But how do we *live* as sacrifices? The offering *died*. Paul calls us to surrender our self-centered motives and live for God instead by following His will and loving others. "We are those who have died to sin. . . . Our old self was crucified with him so that the body ruled by sin might be done away with" (Romans 6:2, 6).

Our willing obedience is more pleasing to God than merely observing religious rituals and traditions without a heart transformation. God longs for our devotion to Him. "Sacrifice and offering you did not desire. . . . Then I said, 'Here I am, I have come. . . . I desire to do your will, my God' " (Psalm 40:6–8). Do you offer yourself fully to God? Is your life a pleasing aroma to Him?

Don't Go It Alone

They devoted themselves to the apostles'
teaching and to fellowship, to the breaking of bread and to prayer.
ACTS 2:42

Generations of men have snickered over this phenomenon: women don't go to the powder room alone. Not only do we need to check our makeup, but we also want counsel and support—or advice to run far and fast from the guy we're with—from the girls we trust the most. And honestly, someone has to reassure us that we don't have food stuck in our teeth.

God created us for relationships—with Him and one another. During Creation the one time God decreed something to be "not good" was when He decided Adam shouldn't be alone. And we're no different today.

Jesus didn't live a lone-ranger existence either. He surrounded Himself with His disciples and friends. He taught them, equipped them, and shared life in their community. He showed by His example that we need to fellowship with other believers.

Sometimes we drift away from regular church attendance and convince ourselves that we're doing fine on our own. But the writer of Hebrews counseled believers in Christ to "not neglect our meeting together, as some people do, but encourage one another" (Hebrews 10:25 NLT).

Outside the community of Christians we can grow weary and, without accountability, might even wander from God's path. It's vital to our spiritual development that we lift one another up, learn, and grow together. "As iron sharpens iron, so one person sharpens another" (Proverbs 27:17). When we're connected with other believers we share each other's burdens, pray for one another, strengthen one another, and accomplish far more together than we ever could alone.

"Many hands make light work" isn't an idle opinion. We require our whole bodies to function properly, and spreading the Good News to the world takes an entire body of believers.

Have you isolated yourself from your sisters and brothers in Christ? Rejoin the group. They need your hands to complete God's work, and you need their encouragement on the journey of discipleship.

That Sinking Feeling

"Can any one of you by worrying add a single hour to your life?"
MATTHEW 6:27

Know any chronic worriers? Or maybe you are one. Life is full of uncertainties and difficulties—there's no lack of upsetting topics to choose from. And while we know that worrying doesn't change anything, we feel compelled to dredge up all the worst-case scenarios and work ourselves right into a nervous breakdown.

But the apostle Peter warns us to be on guard. Satan wants to steal our peace and force us to focus on our fear instead of our faith in God. Worry is really a breakdown of trust in our heavenly Father. "Give all your worries and cares to God, for he cares about you. Stay alert! Watch out for your great enemy, the devil.... Stand firm against him, and be strong in your faith" (1 Peter 5:7–9 NLT).

One night Jesus sent His disciples out onto the Sea of Galilee without Him. The winds were high that night. And just before the sun peeked over the horizon Jesus went for a stroll on the rolling waves. When the disciples saw Him at first they were afraid, but then Peter decided to step out of the boat in faith. He walked on water! But then he made what could have been a disastrous mistake—he took his eyes off Jesus and looked at the raging waves around him. And he started to sink.

When we worry and our faith falters, remember Peter's next action. Realizing he was sinking, he cried out to the only One who could help: "Lord, save me!" (Matthew 14:30). Peter may have lost faith for a moment when he focused on his scary situation, but he quickly realized his mistake.

God is faithful and deserving of our wholehearted trust. Lay your worries at His feet, and "He will cover you with his feathers, and under his wings you will find refuge; his faithfulness will be your shield and rampart" (Psalm 91:4).

When God Says No

But the Lord is faithful. He will establish you.
2 Thessalonians 3:3 esv

Disappointment. You had your heart set, and the path seemed right. Maybe you even thought it was God's will. But suddenly the rug is ripped out from under you. Your fervent prayers seem to bounce off the ceiling. You start to question whether God is listening as the ache of loss seeps into your chest.

Sometimes God's answer is no. It hurts to let go of our wishes, but remember that our loving heavenly Father is in control. Never doubt that God knows your desires. His knowledge is unlimited. "Can a man hide himself in secret places so that I cannot see him? declares the Lord. Do I not fill heaven and earth?" (Jeremiah 23:24 esv). The prophet Jonah played hide-and-seek with God, but the game didn't end well for him. There's nothing like being swallowed by a giant fish to say, "I see you."

God sees His children, and He hears us. Your prayers haven't been swept away. "The eyes of the Lord are on the righteous, and his ears are attentive to their cry" (Psalm 34:15). You have God's attention. And as Jonah discovered, there's no slipping under His radar.

God in His loving wisdom has good reasons for denying our requests:

- He may be protecting us from undetected harm.
- God may have something better planned for us.
- He might be telling us to wait.
- Sin in our lives could be separating us from God.

No one likes to be told no—and often we direct our anger at God. But His no isn't meant as punishment, just as denying a child too much candy isn't done for the sake of meanness. "But we rejoice in our sufferings, knowing that suffering produces endurance, and endurance produces character, and character produces hope. . .because God's love has been poured into our hearts" (Romans 5:3–5 esv). Instead God is lovingly molding us, equipping us, growing us into the wonderful plans He has for us.

Be a Blessing Counter

Every good and perfect gift is from above, coming down from the Father of the heavenly lights, who does not change like shifting shadows.

JAMES 1:17

White Christmas—many people watch and re-watch this classic film as a savored holiday tradition. The Christmas season is a time when we usually think about Jesus' birth and the blessings God has given us. But we shouldn't praise God for all the good gifts He's given us only at Christmastime. It should be a year-round habit.

Sometimes we get so entrenched in our hectic schedules that we don't pause to consider how much God has done for us. We convince ourselves we haven't a second to spare. And we spend the majority of our time focused on what we *don't* have. We find a remedy for our churning thoughts in the smooth, crooning voice of Bing Crosby:

When I'm worried and I can't sleep I count my blessings instead of sheep
And I fall asleep counting my blessings.
When my bankroll is getting small I think of when I had none at all
And I fall asleep counting my blessings.

It's important that we take time each day to acknowledge the blessings that God has given us and thank Him for His provision. It helps us refocus and gain a more balanced perspective. If you are prone to anxiety or negative thoughts, try making a list of all the positive things in your life. Sometimes when we're mired in pessimism it's hard to see the good, so start small. You might be surprised by the number of blessings you've already received. The writer of Hebrews encourages us to "continually offer to God a sacrifice of praise. . . For with such sacrifices God is pleased" (Hebrews 13:15–16).

Do you spend a lot of time comparing yourself to others and complaining about what you don't have? Praise God for the good and perfect gifts He has brought into your life. You'll find your spirits lifted and your heart content. And you'll sleep better too!

A Critical Spirit

Do not let any unwholesome talk come out of your mouths,
but only what is helpful for building others up.
Ephesians 4:29

Perfectionism. It's a toxic attitude that often masquerades as a desirable quality. Being a high achiever is great, but when we refuse to accept anything less than perfection, instead of making us better and helping us reach our goals, it erodes our self-esteem and our ability to trust others. It's a ticket to unhappiness that's usually accompanied by depression. Perfectionists find it hard to see the good in other people's efforts. Instead they hone in on the tiniest flaws and become overly critical of themselves and everyone around them. Judgmental and defensive, their prickly personalities aren't fun to be around.

Romans 12:3 (NLT) warns, "Don't think you are better than you really are." The reality is that none of us is perfect. We will fail, and we will make mistakes. But perfectionism tricks us into worshipping the idol of self. I can do it better. If you want it done right, do it yourself. We become obsessive about control and criticize every effort others make while pointing out their smallest mistakes. And worse yet, we can't escape our own judgment.

The problem is we've put our focus in the wrong place. Instead of trembling at the thought of failure, we should be "fixing our eyes on Jesus, the pioneer and perfecter of faith" (Hebrews 12:2). We need to release our death grip on control and allow Jesus to do the perfecting. The Lord assures us, "My grace is sufficient for you, for my power is made perfect in weakness" (2 Corinthians 12:9).

Do you notice any seeds of perfectionism taking root in your life? Do you think whatever you accomplish is never quite good enough? Are you ruthlessly critical? If so, allow your heavenly Father to reclaim His throne. Recognize that He alone is in control. "For I am confident of this very thing, that He who began a good work in you will perfect it until the day of Christ Jesus" (Philippians 1:6 NASB).

Patience, Please

God waited patiently in the days of Noah while the ark was being built.

1 PETER 3:20

"She has some nerve," Liz whispers to Amy when their friend Meredith slips into the pew in front of them. "She wasn't raised that way. How can she live like that and then show her face here?"

Patience is a quality that only the Holy Spirit can cultivate. But the patience referred to in Galatians 5 isn't the kind we use when we're experiencing difficulties; instead it's the variety God offers His children—the same patience we should have toward one another.

The apostle Paul said, "I was shown mercy so that in me, the worst of sinners, Christ Jesus might display his immense patience as an example for those who would believe in him and receive eternal life" (1 Timothy 1:16). Paul called himself the worst sinner, yet God, motivated by mercy, has great patience with His wayward children because He wants us all to come to Him and receive His gift of eternal life. The apostle Peter reminds us that "our Lord's patience means salvation" (2 Peter 3:15).

Because God is patient He offers us mercy, and He expects us to follow His lead: "Be patient and stand firm.... Don't grumble against one another, brothers and sisters, or you will be judged" (James 5:8–9). Patience doesn't mean we accept sin, but it does carry the added responsibility of not condemning one another. "So when you, a mere human being, pass judgment on them and yet do the same things, do you think you will escape God's judgment? Or do you show contempt for the riches of his kindness, forbearance and patience, not realizing that God's kindness is intended to lead you to repentance?" (Romans 2:3–4). God withholds His judgment to bring us back to Him.

When you're tempted to point a convicting finger, remember that "because of the LORD's great love we are not consumed, for his compassions never fail" (Lamentations 3:22). Instead, reserve your judgment and apply some patience.

166

Need Some Light?

Your word is a lamp for my feet, a light on my path.
PSALM 119:105

The wind howls with furious force outside your door. The lights flicker and blink out. Darkness surrounds you. Even though you've walked through your house thousands of times, you still crack your shins on the coffee table and trip over a chair on your way to find a flashlight. It's easy to stumble when you can't see where you're going.

God gave us His Word for the same reason we flip the light switch at night—to illuminate our paths. We have boatloads of excuses for why we can't spend time studying our Bibles daily, but when we convince ourselves that we're too busy or it's too hard to understand scripture anyway, we're only handicapping ourselves by hanging out in the dark.

Instead we should adopt the attitude of the first-century Christians: "They received the message with great eagerness and examined the Scriptures every day to see if what Paul said was true" (Acts 17:11). Going to church and listening to sermons is important for growing spiritually, but we also have to read God's Word for ourselves so we won't be led astray.

Satan is a trickster. He relishes every opportunity to trip us up. But when the father of lies tried to bamboozle Jesus in the desert, Jesus answered with three little words: "it is written." When we're tempted to stray or unsure about what we should do, we need reinforcements. "I have hidden your word in my heart that I might not sin against you" (Psalm 119:11). It's a lot easier to see the devil's traps when you're walking in the light of God's Word. "The law of their God is in their hearts; their feet do not slip" (Psalm 37:31).

Where is your Bible right now? Do you know? Is it coated with dust? Pick it up so God can light up your life.

Secret of Contentment

I am not saying this because I am in need,
for I have learned to be content whatever the circumstances.
PHILIPPIANS 4:11

What does it mean to be content? It's not really something the world preaches. Instead we're flooded with commercials, advertisements, and billboards whose sole purpose is to convince us we can't live without something we didn't know we needed five minutes ago. Success is measured in square footage and the number of toys we accumulate. Like mice on a wheel we run after more, bigger, and better never to arrive—something more impressive always comes along.

The American Heritage Dictionary defines contentment as "desiring no more than what one has; satisfied." What a relief it would be to get out of the rat race and simply be satisfied. But how do we capture this elusive state?

The apostle Paul shared his secret to being content, even though he was sitting in a Roman prison when he wrote it. "I know what it is to be in need, and I know what it is to have plenty. I have learned the secret of being content in any and every situation, whether well fed or hungry, whether living in plenty or in want. I can do all this through him who gives me strength" (Philippians 4:12–13).

Paul learned to rely on Christ to supply his needs and give him strength instead of the things society peddles. He changed his focus from this world to the next—and to the One who had provided for his eternal retirement. Paul praised God instead of thinking about what he lacked. "Rejoice in the Lord always. I will say it again: Rejoice!" (Philippians 4:4).

We too can rely on God's power and His promises. He offers strength, protection, and peace. Trust in Christ as Paul did. And discover the secret to living a life of contentment. "Peace I leave with you; my peace I give you. I do not give to you as the world gives. Do not let your hearts be troubled" (John 14:27).

Refined by Fire

*In this you rejoice, even if now for a little while you have had to suffer various
trials, so that the genuineness of your faith—being more precious than gold
that, though perishable, is tested by fire—may be found to result in
praise and glory and honor when Jesus Christ is revealed.*

1 PETER 1:6–7 NRSV

W hy do good people suffer? It's a question of the ages. Job was proclaimed
by God to be "blameless and upright, a man who fears God and shuns evil"
(Job 1:8). And yet he suffered both emotional and physical torment. Job was
also a very wealthy man. He had seven sons and three daughters, seven thousand
sheep, three thousand camels, five hundred yoke of oxen, five hundred donkeys,
and many servants. Job 1:3 tells us that "he was the greatest man among all the
people of the East."

But in a single day Satan obliterated everything, Job's children, livestock,
and servants—gone. Yet through his pain Job answered, "The LORD gave and
the LORD has taken away; may the name of the LORD be praised" (Job 1:21).

But Satan again petitioned God and was permitted to afflict Job further with
painful sores. He had lost his health, his family, and his possessions, and yet "in
all this, Job did not sin in what he said" (Job 2:10).

It's tempting to view suffering as abandonment by God or punishment for
wrongdoing. But the book of Job offers us insight into the loving provision of our
heavenly Father, who sees our hearts and our eternal future. The trials and suffering of believers in Christ are evidence of God's love rather than His punishment.

As the pain of a surgeon's scalpel can save a cancer patient's life, God uses
suffering to refine our righteousness. He uses our discomfort to bring us understanding and trust in Him that can't be learned another way—to save rather than
to punish. We should look for our Creator's refining work through our pain.

Christlike

Therefore be imitators of God, as beloved children; and walk in love, just as Christ also loved you and gave Himself up for us, an offering and a sacrifice to God as a fragrant aroma.

EPHESIANS 5:1–2 NASB

———————

Mahatma Gandhi is often quoted as saying, "I like your Christ, I do not like your Christians. Your Christians are so unlike your Christ." Unfortunately many people in our own culture share his opinion—often with good reason. Many modern believers have become mere pew-sitters, going to church every Sunday and calling themselves by the name "Christian," but failing to allow Christ to change the way they think and act throughout the rest of the week. We say that we believe Jesus died for our sins and gave us the mind-boggling gift of eternal life, but have we allowed this life-altering knowledge to do its work? Do our lives look any different from our unbelieving neighbors'?

The apostle Peter challenged the church to "get rid of all evil behavior. Be done with all deceit, hypocrisy, jealousy, and all unkind speech. Like newborn babies, you must crave pure spiritual milk so that you will grow into a full experience of salvation. Cry out for this nourishment, now that you have had a taste of the Lord's kindness" (1 Peter 2:1–3 NLT). Do we crave spiritual nourishment? Once we've experienced that first taste of the goodness of God we should be crying out for Christ to show us more about living in love as He did.

It's time to grow up in our salvation. Becoming followers of Christ should affect everything we do and think and say. But for this to happen we must first put Christ in the center of our lives. Peter cautioned the church to "abstain from sinful desires, which wage war against your soul. Live such good lives among the pagans that, though they accuse you of doing wrong, they may see your good deeds and glorify God" (1 Peter 2:11–12).

So put on your big-girl pants. God is calling you to action.

Goodbye, Gloomy Gus

Praise the LORD, my soul, and forget not all his benefits.
PSALM 103:2

❖━━━❖━━━❖━━━❖

Do you know any irritatingly chipper people? Just when you want to have a nice wallow in self-pity, you run into one of those glass-half-full types who seem to have wholeheartedly embraced the slogan "Always look on the bright side." And they're out to spread sunshine over your rainy parade.

Perhaps we do need to exchange our negativity for a positive outlook. The apostle Paul closed his letter to the Thessalonian believers with just such advice. "Rejoice always, pray continually, give thanks in all circumstances; for this is God's will for you in Christ Jesus" (1 Thessalonians 5:16–18). Adopting this motto would certainly revitalize a dreary perspective.

Now don't think that living this way means we go around with silly grins on our faces all the time. We are guaranteed to go through difficult times, but we have joy because our heavenly Father is in control and uses our struggles to refine our faith.

And we obviously can't spend 24-7 on our knees. What God desires is a relationship with us. That requires communication. Nurturing a prayerful attitude involves recognizing our need for God and resting in His constant presence in our lives.

And last, Paul doesn't say to be thankful *for* all things, he says to give thanks *in* all things. God doesn't cause evil, and we aren't expected to thank Him for bad things that happen to us. But regardless of our circumstances, God is there. And He can use our situation to accomplish His good.

God loves us, and He has big plans for each of us. He doesn't call us to live in anxiety, fear, and pessimism, but in trust. "Trust in the LORD with all your heart; do not depend on your own understanding. Seek his will in all you do, and he will show you which path to take" (Proverbs 3:5–6 NLT).

Imagine the change we'd bring by living in a state of joy, prayer, and thankfulness.

Driven with the Wind

By faith we understand that the universe was formed at God's command.
HEBREWS 11:3

Thomas wasn't about to be taken in by unconfirmed reports. His ten friends told him that Jesus had risen from the dead, but Thomas wasn't convinced. "Unless I see the nail marks in his hands and put my finger where the nails were, and put my hand into his side, I will not believe" (John 20:25).

Let's not be too hard on Thomas. Most of us struggle with doubt from time to time. We doubt God's promises, His character, and even His very existence. We question His love for us when things go wrong. But Thomas was a true follower of Christ. Famous for his doubts, his courage and devotion to Jesus are often overlooked. Knowing that accompanying Jesus to Jerusalem could mean his death, the intrepid Thomas said, "Let us also go, that we may die with him" (John 11:16).

Thomas may have had reservations about Jesus coming back to life, but once his questions were answered, he moved on to faith and belief. After he had felt the nail holes in Jesus' hands, he said, "My Lord and my God!" (John 20:28). He didn't allow his doubt to become a permanent condition.

Our doubts should lead us to find answers that strengthen our belief. Thomas took his concerns to Jesus and his faith was confirmed. If we become caught in a state of doubt, we're likely restless and open to suggestion. We lack the confident assurance of faith. "For he that wavereth is like a wave of the sea driven with the wind and tossed" (James 1:6 KJV).

While we don't have the opportunity to see Jesus physically, He promised that "blessed are those who have not seen and yet have believed" (John 20:29). When doubts trouble us, we can pray for "confidence in what we hope for and assurance about what we do not see" (Hebrews 11:1).

Do you allow your doubts to strand you in the rolling waves of uncertainty, or do they prod you toward spiritual growth?

Skin Deep

Charm is deceitful, and beauty is vain,
but a woman who fears the LORD is to be praised.
PROVERBS 31:30 ESV

What does an idol look like? It's usually a figure, probably made of wood, stone, or a precious metal. It's placed in a prominent place and people bow down to worship it. Right? Well. . .sometimes. The things we idolize today aren't always so readily recognizable. One in particular can be dazzlingly subtle—the god of self.

Society is increasingly mindful of outward appearance, especially for women. We're under extreme pressure to have that sculpted body, a flawless face, the designer wardrobe, and salon-perfect hair. And many have succumbed to the narcissism of self-worship. Enamored with themselves, their sole purpose is impressing others with their external perfection.

Health and fitness aren't evil. It's good to take care of ourselves, but when we neglect our inner, spiritual growth and buy into the lie that our worth is determined by our looks, it's hard to reflect Jesus. The apostle Paul explained that "physical training is of some value, but godliness has value for all things, holding promise for both the present life and the life to come" (1 Timothy 4:8). All the primping in the world can't affect our eternal value.

God once chastised His prophet Samuel for trying to judge the future king of Israel based on appearance: "Do not consider his appearance or his height, for I have rejected him. . . . People look at the outward appearance, but the LORD looks at the heart" (1 Samuel 16:7).

"Do not let your adorning be external—the braiding of hair and the putting on of gold jewelry, or the clothing you wear—but let your adorning be the hidden person of the heart with the imperishable beauty of a gentle and quiet spirit, which in God's sight is very precious" (1 Peter 3:3–4 ESV). What's in your heart? Does God see someone so preoccupied with appearance that she's neglected her spirit? Or is your heart beautiful to Him?

Sweet Dreams

"Be strong and courageous. Do not be afraid; do not be discouraged,
for the LORD your God will be with you wherever you go."

JOSHUA 1:9

❦

Kids are often afraid of the dark. Sometimes they crawl into bed with Mom and Dad, and sometimes they huddle in their blankets, trying not to see monsters in the shadows of their closets. Once we're caught in the irrational, gripping clutches of fear, it's hard to get loose.

But fear isn't only a childhood malady. As adults we may not check under our beds before going to sleep, but anxiety and fear can still plague our minds. What if you lose your job in the upcoming cutbacks? What if your recent medical tests come back showing cancer? How will you provide for your family?

God watches over His children. He knows everything that is happening in your life. Jesus promised, "Are not two sparrows sold for a penny? Yet not one of them will fall to the ground outside your Father's care. And even the very hairs of your head are all numbered. So don't be afraid; you are worth more than many sparrows" (Matthew 10:29–31). God notices when even a little bird falls, and He values us far above His feathered creations. We are worth so much to Him that He sent His Son to die in our place. "For God so loved the world that he gave his one and only Son, that whoever believes in him shall not perish but have eternal life" (John 3:16).

When anxiety closes in you have two choices—be ruled by fear or choose to trust in the One who loves you most. "When I am afraid, I put my trust in you. In God, whose word I praise—in God I trust and am not afraid. What can mere mortals do to me?" (Psalm 56:3–4). Trust your heavenly Father; release your fears to His care. And "when you lie down, you will not be afraid. . .your sleep will be sweet" (Proverbs 3:24).

Watch Out!

Do not let sin reign in your mortal body.
ROMANS 6:12

In ancient times iron tools were definitely an improvement over wood and stone, but iron still has weaknesses—it bends and loses a sharp edge quickly. But iron can be enhanced. By removing its impurities and reheating it in a furnace with charcoal (carbon), some of the carbon combines with the iron, producing steel. Steel can be a thousand times stronger than iron in its pure form.

Because of our impurities we also have certain weaknesses and propensities—maybe even cherished sins. But we often don't recognize our own shortcomings. That's why it's so important for us to study God's Word. We need a better standard than our own. "I would not have known what sin was had it not been for the law" (Romans 7:7). If you have never seen the light, it's impossible to know you're stuck in the dark.

We also have to be on guard. "Stay alert! Watch out for your great enemy, the devil." (1 Peter 5:8 NLT). Satan has been studying human nature since time began. He knows how we operate and delights in leading us away from God.

But Satan doesn't always have to convince us. "Each person is tempted when they are dragged away by their own evil desire and enticed" (James 1:14). We're pretty good at persuading ourselves that we're comfortable, that change is unnecessary. It's not our first inclination to do things that aren't fun. We enjoy the sins we gravitate toward. We revel in our arrogance or savor juicy gossip. We exult in the admiring glances of others or uphold our illusion of control through our worries.

Iron isn't strong in its natural ore. Something must be added and something removed. When we become believers in Christ the Holy Spirit takes up residence in us and transforms us by replacing our sinful desires with the fruit of the Spirit. But stay on your toes! Satan and your own desires can lead you astray.

Venture Outside the Camp

He [Moses] regarded disgrace for the sake of Christ as of greater value than the
treasures of Egypt, because he was looking ahead to his reward.
HEBREWS 11:26

A tiger can't change his stripes. We often hear that we're stuck with our essential disposition. Nature and nurture have conditioned us toward certain behaviors. And despite our numerous New Year's resolutions and promises to change for the better, we usually slide back into familiar routines. We like to stay comfortable.

After Jesus' death, some Hebrew Christians were ridiculed for giving up the old ways of sacrifice, and many were slipping back into their familiar traditions. But the writer of Hebrews urged them to leave behind their old habits and "go to [Jesus] outside the camp, bearing the disgrace he bore" (Hebrews 13:13).

This verse refers to the Old Testament practice of burning sin offerings outside the camp. "All the rest of the bull—he must take outside the camp. . .and burn it there" (Leviticus 4:12).

But Jesus fulfilled the Old Testament law and wiped out the sacrificial system with His own blood. He is the perfect Lamb who was taken outside the city and crucified as the bearer of our sins. Jesus said, " 'Here I am, I have come to do your will.' . . . And by that will, we have been made holy through the sacrifice of the body of Jesus Christ once for all" (Hebrews 10:9–10).

As believers in Christ we are to leave our past sinful behavior behind, although it might mean enduring scorn for standing out from the crowd. It's true a tiger can't alter his coat, but God has given us the Holy Spirit to help and teach us. And He promises that "if anyone is in Christ, he is a new creation" (2 Corinthians 5:17 ESV).

Have you settled into what is convenient and comfortable? Did your actions, thoughts, and attitudes change when you met Jesus? Give yourself completely to Him and join Jesus outside the camp.

Additional Notes